1. The tallest person to ever live that didn't suffer from gigantism was Angus MacAskill. He was 7ft 9.

2. The pigs in Angry Birds were inspired by Swine Flu.

3. Crazy golf was only invented to stop women from playing real golf because men were worried that a woman's undergarments would be indecently exposed when she swung her club. The first crazy golf course was created in 1867 in Scotland. It was called St. Andrews' Ladies Putting Club.

4. The word "hyphenated" is not hyphenated. The word "non-hyphenated" is hyphenated.

5. Antarctica is nearly twice the size of Australia.

6. Every year, Americans throw away 141 trillion calories of food. That's enough to feed 200 million people (the amount of homeless people that live in China) three meals a day for a year.

7. Mormons are not allowed to swim or have hot drinks. Also, they are only allowed to play basketball on a half-court.

8. In 2015, the three largest banks made $6 billion from ATM and overdraft fees.

9. The chances of getting a royal flush in poker is 1 in 649,739.

10. The island of Saint Helena has maintained its economy through one main export – stamps. Saint Helena is a tiny, isolated island that has great difficulty managing imports and exports. However, none of that matters to eccentric billionaires who obsessively collect every stamp in the world. The people of Saint Helena take advantage of this by constantly printing new stamps for outrageous prices, knowing that someone will buy them. Because Saint Helena is so inaccessible, buyers are more willing to spend ludicrous money, worried that someone else might beat them to it on stamps. Because of this, Saint Helena has been financially self-sufficient since 1980.

11. In 2001, the European Union ruled that tomatoes, rhubarb,

carrots, and sweet potatoes are fruits. They are considered vegetables everywhere else in the world.

12. One gram of DNA can contain 700 terabytes of data. That's 400,000 times more data than the average laptop.

13. At the ocean's deepest point, the water pressure is the same as having 50 jumbo jets piled on top of you.

14. Only 12 people on Earth have dived lower than 790ft.

15. A man on Kickstarter asked for $10 so he could make potato salad. He raised $55,492.

16. Grapes will explode if they are cooked in a microwave.

17. 2,500 Americans will try cocaine for the first time today.

18. The female for "dude" is "dudine."

19. It takes 17 million barrels of oil annually to make water bottles for the US.

20. A chicken nugget was sold on eBay for $8,100 because it looked like George Washington.

21. Thomas Ferebee is the name of the pilot who dropped the first atomic bomb on Japan.

22. A man memorized the French dictionary to win the French Scrabble Championship. He doesn't speak French.

23. Gymnasium means "school for naked exercise."

24. Apple have so much money, they could bail out Greece twice and still have $2 billion left.

25. Approximately 7% of all wars in history were religiously motivated.

26. Only once in history has a submarine deliberately sunk another submerged submarine.

27. The Aztecs used to sacrifice 250,000 of their people annually.

28. In the last 3,400 years, humans have been at peace for 268 years. That's 8% of recorded history.

29. 80% of all marriages in history were between second cousins or closer.

30. Mexican general, Santa Anna, had a state funeral for his amputated leg.

31. Although Vikings never used skulls as cups, Britons did during the Ice Age.

32. The eruption of Krakatoa in 1883 was the loudest sound in recorded history. It could be heard from 3,000 miles away.

33. Florence Lawrence was the first famous film actress. She was also the first actor to have her name in the opening credits. She appeared in over 200 silent films.

34. There is a 300-page book called A Void that doesn't use the letter "e" once.

35. The foam that appears on shampoo, toothpaste, soap, and other cleaning products has no function. It's only put into cleaning products because consumers associate it with quality.

36. Ozzy Osborne has an overactive ADH4 gene which makes him have an absurdly high tolerance to marijuana, opiates, and methamphetamines.

37. The football huddle was invented by an all-deaf team at Gallaudet so opposing teams couldn't see them performing sign language.

38. Some bananas are pink. When they become ripe, they peel themselves.

39. Hershey's Kisses are so-called because the machine that makes them looks like it's kissing the conveyor belt.

40. The National Academy of Science provide free counsel for moviemakers to make films and television more scientifically accurate.

41. There are over 65,000 iPhones apps, with dozens of new ones created every day.

42. There's a 3% chance that a person will completely recover from CPR treatment after three months.

43. Travis Durden is a French artist who combines the heads of Star Wars characters with the bodies of Greek statues.

44. Your birthday is the most likely day you will die.

45. The average person drinks 16,000 gallons throughout their lifetime.

46. Emerson Moser is the creator of Crayons. He was color-blind.

47. An Indian criminal called Behram has the world record for killing the most people with his bare hands. He personally strangled 931 people between 1790-1840.

48. 111,111,111 x 111,111,111 = 12,345,678,987,654,321.

49. The designer of the Titanic, Thomas Andrews, was on the ship when it sank. He wanted the vessel to have twice as many lifeboats but was overruled. He was last seen helping evacuating passengers of the ship. He died on the Titanic and his body was never recovered.

50. What do the following paintings have in common? -
       The Crucifixion of Christ (1350)
       The Baptism of Christ (1710)
       Madonna with Saint Giovannino (1400s)
    If you said they all reference the Bible, you are correct. But they have something else in common. There is a UFO in each painting.

51. In 2009, a French submarine and a British submarine collided

into each other in the Atlantic. Neither one of them detected each other.

52. Computer Science was the first arcade game ever. It was released in 1971.

53. The Catholic Church considered the theory of evolution to be "virtually certain."

54. Some customers at Disneyland hire disabled people for $130 per hour to cut in line so they don't have to queue.

55. Samsung has an app called Family Hub Fridge that takes a picture of the inside of your fridge every time you open it. If you go to the grocery store and forget what you were supposed to buy, you can check your app and it will tell you.

56. One share of Coca-Cola stock purchased in 1919 for $40 is now worth $9.8 million today.

57. A US Navy research vessel was designed to function even if it is capsized vertically. Because of this, most of the rooms have a vertical and a horizontal door so the crew can walk around like normal even if the ship is capsized.

58. According to Google, the search for "how to roll a joint" peaks between 1am and 2am.

59. Petroleum is the most valuable traded commodity in the world.

60. The webcam was invented in Cambridge to check the status of a coffee pot.

61. The technology behind smartphones relies on 250,000 separate patents.

62. 80% of all Soviet males born in 1923 died during World War II.

63. SEAL Team Six was named to confuse its enemies. When it was created, there were only two members on the team. When enemies saw the two members, they were distracted, looking for the other four members even though they didn't exist.

64. Dolph Lundgren is musclebound actor who is most famous for playing Ivan Drago in Rocky IV. Years ago, three masked men broke into his house and tied up his wife. They started to steal objects in the house until they saw a picture of Dolph. Once they realized whose house they were stealing from, they dropped everything and ran away.

65. Approximately 107 billion have lived on Earth. 40% of them died before they were one year old.

66. Instant coffee was invented in 1910 by a man called George Washington.

67. Nazi minister of propaganda, Joseph Goebbels, targeted people who had physical abnormalities. He himself had a deformed leg.

68. Pantelligent is a frying pan that sends messages to your phone that tell you the temperature of the food, when to stir, change the heat, etc.

69. Billy Wyman was 52 when he married 18-year-old Mandy Smith. They got divorced a year later. Billy's 30-year-old son, Stephen, then married Mandy's 46-year-old mother. If Billy and Mandy didn't get divorced, Stephen would've been his own grandfather!!!

70. Mark Spitz was a nine-time Olympic champion. When the Russian swim team coach asked him how he was so skillful, he jokingly said it was because of his moustache. The following year, every Russian swimmer on the team had a moustache.

71. Hookah has 25 times more tar, ten times more carbon monoxide, and nearly three times more nicotine than a cigarette.

72. In 1980, Maureen Wilcox picked the correct numbers for the Massachusetts lottery and the Rhode Island lottery. However, she didn't win any money because she played the winning numbers for each lottery on the other ticket!

73. Salt is used for de-icing roads more than for human

consumption.

74. Radivoke Lajic's house was destroyed after it got hit by a meteorite... SIX TIMES! That's six separate meteorites hitting the exact same house on six different occasions.

75. Andre the Giant drank 127 beers in a row. Unsurprisingly, he passed out. He had a NYPD officer with him to make sure he didn't fall on anyone while drunk.

76. If officials awarded Lance Armstrong's 2005 Tour De France title to the next finisher who didn't take enhancing drugs, the award would've went to the person who finished in 23rd place.

77. There is a wearable noise-cancelling device called Silent Partner. When it is put on your nose, it creates a soundwave that cancels out whatever noise you're making. It's been used for snoring.

78. You are more likely to be killed by a champagne cork than a spider.

79. Jackie Chan had eyelid surgery in 1976 to look more "Western," hoping to get more acting work in America. The last film he appeared in with his original look was the 1976 movie, Shaolin Wooden Men.

80. The first film with a narrative was the 1903 film, The Great Train Robbery. Although it was just over 11 minutes long, it was also one of the first films to have editing.

81. Penicillin was so rare in the 1930s, it was re-extracted from the urine of patients.

82. A commercially successful film is known as a "blockbuster." However, it used to be a term for an aerial bomb that was so powerful, it could destroy or "bust" an entire block.

83. A Polish composer died in 1982 and left his body to science except his skull, which he donated to the Royal Shakespeare Company so he could be used as a prop in Hamlet.

84. On the 10-piece Chicken McNugget box at McDonalds, there is a picture of 11 nuggets.

85. In 1959, pilot Lt. Colonel William Rankin ejected from his plane during a thunderstorm. The weather was so violent he didn't hit the ground for 40 minutes.

86. Louise Pasteur worked on the rabies vaccine. He told his staff if anyone were to be infected with the virus, including himself, he or she was to be shot in the head.

87. Hitler's Third Reich awarded the Cross of the German Mother to women who gave birth to 13 children.

88. The children's book, Where the Wild Things Are, was supposed to be called Where the Wild Horses Are until the writer realized he couldn't draw horses.

89. In 2010, the Catholic Church had an income of $97 billion.

90. Humanity figured out how to put a man on the Moon before anyone thought of putting wheels on suitcases.

91. The 1900 Olympics had "sports" such as kite-flying, painting, town-planning, sculpting, poetry, and firefighting. Also, croquet used to be an Olympic event. There was one spectator in the audience.

92. Pacific Avenue is the most valuable property in the board game, Monopoly. The chances of landing on it on your first turn are 0.028%.

93. Four skeletons dating back to 4400 BC were discovered in Eulau, Germany. The skeletons were of a man, woman, and their two children. The female skeleton was clutching the hand of one of her children. This is the oldest complete human family ever found.

94. There's less than an 8% chance that a coin flipped 100 times will land 50 times on Tails and 50 times on Heads.

95. The very first face to appear on Facebook was of Al Pacino.

96. All the mined gold on Earth can fit in a 20x20x20 meter cube.

97. A martial arts sensei doesn't need to be a black belt or have any sort of license to be a qualified instructor.

98. Bruce Willis was the first actor to act in a video game. He starred in the 1998 game, Apocalypse.

99. Coffee means "wind of the bean."

100.   2,520 is the smallest number that can be exactly divided by all the numbers from 1 to 10.

101.   There are keyboards designed to sound like typewriters when the keys are tapped.

102.   If you could type 60 words per minute, eight hours per day, it would take 50 years to write the human genome.

103.   The winds in Antarctica can get up to 200mph.

104.   A jewel heist occurred in a German museum called the Kaufhaus des Westens. The police did a DNA test and found the culprit. However, they learned the culprit had an identical twin. Since they were identical, their DNA was the same. Neither man was charged as there was no way to figure out which one was the criminal.

105.   There are radar detectors that use radar detector detector detectors to detect radar detector detectors. And why do they do this? To avoid detection.

106.   A tramp is someone who only works when he has to. A bum is someone who doesn't work. A hobo is someone that has to travel to find work.

107.   Until recently, geneticists believed that white-skinned humans became common place approximately 40,000 years ago. However, new evidence was discovered in 2014 that revealed that white-skinned humans have only existed for 7,000 years at most.

108. Wouldn't it be cool to be a bounty hunter? Not really, since the Supreme Court has decided that anyone can say they are a bounty hunter without a license, diploma, or any form of training.

109. In 1994, a 75lb bag of cocaine fell out of a plane and landed in a Florida crime watch meeting.

110. If you search for "Askew" in Google, the content will tilt to one side.

111. Robert Watson-Watt invented radar. Years later, he was caught speeding with a radar gun. He then said, "If I'd known what they were going to do with it, I'd have never have invented it."

112. German interrogator, Hanns Scharff, worked a POW (Prisoners of War) camp. However, he refused to torture the prisoners and instead, went for a walk with them or buy them lunch. They revealed information to him without him relying on threats or violence. After the war, he moved to America and became an artist.

113. Judge Judy makes $45 million annually. She works 52 days per year.

114. The most passengers to get on a single plane is 1,086. However, 1088 got off the plane because two women gave birth.

115. Of the top 50 most successful films of all time, 47 of them are sequels, reboots, prequels, or based on a novel. Only three of them are original pieces of work.

116. "Desperation" is an anagram of "a rope ends it."

117. In the 1980s, IMSAI were selling a computer that could hold 10MB. That's approximately 100,000 times less than what a conventional computer can hold today. The product cost $5,995.

118. A detective called Tim Dohr caught a criminal that was hiding in a building by playing the game, Marco Polo. When Dohr shouted "Marco," the criminal instinctively said "Polo" and was caught.

119. On January 29th 2015, Professor David Nutt committed a survey to see what people believed was the most dangerous drug. 97% of people believed that most drug deaths are caused by heroin. In fact, 72% drug deaths involve alcohol.

120. If science contradicts religion according to Buddism, the religious beliefs are deemed incorrect.

121. Although the first Thanksgiving was in 1621, 19th century Women's Magazine's editor, Sarah Hale, devised the Thanksgiving meal that Americans eat today. It was also her idea for making the Christmas tree synonymous with Christmas. On top of that, she wrote the poem, Mary Had A Little Lamb.

122. A lot of junk is thrown into the sea. So how long does it take for garbage to dissolve in the ocean?
   i)   Plastic bag – 15 years
   ii) Styrofoam cup – 50 years
   iii) Can – 200 years
   iv) Plastic beverage holder – 400 years
   v)   Plastic bottle – 450 years
   vi) Diaper – 450 years
   vii) Fishing Line – 600 years

123. Rosalind Franklin was an x-ray crystallographer who discovered the structure of DNA. Due to overexposure to x-rays in her career, she died of cancer. Her business partners, James Watson, Francis Crick, and Maurice Wilkins picked up the Nobel Prize for her work. Her name wasn't even mentioned. It's also worth mentioning that Watson firmly believed that stupidity was a disease.

124. How much would it cost to build Jurassic Park? Well, to buy the two islands that the Park resides in would cost $10 billion alone. The park itself would cost $1.5 billion. Including operational costs, food, workers, etc. the grand total would be

$23.4 billion and an extra $11.9 billion every year to maintain the park. And that's not even including the dinosaurs. I can't really run potential costs on them since cloning dinosaurs is purely theoretical.

125.   The Bible is the most shoplifted book in the world.

126.   Facebook tracks which sites you visit, even after you have signed out.

127.   The St. Cuthbert Gospel is the world's oldest paper book. It dates back to the 7th century.

128.   In April 2013, someone hacked Associated Press' Twitter account and tweeted that two bombs had exploded at the White House. The Stock Market crashed within seconds.

129.   March 14th 2015 at 9:26:53 make up the first ten digits of pi – 3.141592653.

130.   The average lead pencil can write 50,000 English words.

131.   Mother's Day wasn't created to celebrate mothers but was a Christian celebration called Mothering Sunday. Christians saw the church as their "mother" and went to church on this day. The holiday didn't celebrate motherhood until the early 20th century. Anna Jarvis, who devised Mother's Day, grew to despise the holiday, mainly because greeting cards "mean nothing except that you are too lazy to write to the woman who has done more for you than anyone in the world."

132.   International Women's Day is the most common day of the year when people search for "International Men's Day" online. In case you're wondering, International Men's Day is November 19th.

133.   "Gadzooks" is a word people originally used as a substitute for using the Lord's name in vain. "Gadzooks" actually means "God's hooks" and relates to the nails in Christ's palms and the crowns on his head.

134.   Ronald Wayne sold his 10% stake in Apple for $800. It is

now worth $58,065,210,000.

135. David Edward Hughes invented a radio before radio waves were discovered. He never tried to develop his invention because his colleagues dismissed his claims.

136. During the WWI and WWII, hundreds of ships were painted in black-and-white stripes so enemy forces couldn't tell the size or type of ship it was. However, these colorful ships were far more visible and were detected almost instantly.

137. Wings was the first film to win a Best Picture Oscar in 1927. It also had the first same-sex kiss in movie history.

138. The first parody film was The Little Train Robbery in 1905. It was a remake of the 1903 film, The Great Train Robbery, except all the cast were children.

139. 123-45-67+89=100.
123+4-5+67-89=100.
123-4-5-6-7+8+9=100.
1+23-4+5+6+78-9=100.

140. Some Holocaust survivors died within the first week of freedom after overdosing on chocolate.

141. Just before Gary Gilmore was sentenced to death, he said, "Just do it." Nike decided to use these words as their slogan.

142. 71% of convicted violent criminals in the US will be arrested for new crimes within five years of being released from prison.

143. 12-13% of homeless adults in the US are veterans (57,000.)

144. The most common currency in American prisons is Ramen noodles.

145. While making video games, developers will sometimes add blatantly bad features to distract their managers from game-crashing bugs they have yet to fix.

146. An art professor from Syracuse University created a single

tree that bared 40 different types of fruit.

147. During WWI, it was considered unlucky to be the third person to light a cigarette. Soldiers reasoned that the enemy saw the first light, took aim at the second, and shot at the third.

148. The app, Wakie, allows you to personally record an alarm for a total stranger.

149. The Twilight series has sold almost double the Game of Thrones series, His Dark Materials series, and The Dark Tower series combined.

150. Bibliomancy is the practice of opening the Bible at random to guide oneself by whatever verse is read first.

151. When the incredibly wealthy Maharaja of Patiala visited a Roll Royce showroom, he asked how much a car cost. The salesman had no idea who he was speaking to so he told the Maharaja that he couldn't afford it. To spite the salesman, the Maharaja bought every single car in the showroom, cut the roofs off, and turned them into garbage trucks.

152. Jay Z, The Notorious BIG, Busta Rhymes, and DMX went to the same high school before they became famous rappers.

153. Smoking one cigarette reduces your life span by 11 minutes.

154. The first computer-generated character was in the television series, Young Sherlock Holmes, in 1985. The effect was created by John Lasseter. He is the director of Toy Story.

155. 65 million neutrinos pass through your thumbnail every second. A neutrino is a subatomic particle. If an atom was the size of the Solar System, a neutrino would be the size of a golf ball.

156. There is an AI unit that makes telemarketers believe they are speaking to a real person, just to waste their time.

157. There's a town in Scotland called Dull. There's a town in Oregon called Boring. There's a town in Australia called Bland.

They are known as The Trinity of Tedium.

158.   Everything is made of atoms. Therefore, a scientist studying atoms is just a bunch of atoms studying itself.

159.   Most people know that atoms are mainly made of empty space. But how much empty space? Well, if all the empty space was removed from the atoms that make up every human on Earth, the population of the world could fit inside an apple.

160.   Between November 2012 through December 2013, 2,259 peer-review articles about global warming were studied by 9,136 climatologists. After studying the articles, only one climatologist believed that global warming is a myth.
   Despite the fact that some people believe global warming is a hoax, there is more CO_2 in the atmosphere than at any point in the last 800,000 years.
   According to the American Association for the Advancement of Science, there is more proof that humans are causing global warming than smoking causes lung cancer.

161.   Duct tape is awful at sealing ducts. However, duct tape is surprisingly effective against warts.

162.   Thiomargarita namibiensis is the largest bacteria, measuring 0.75mm. It's so big, you can see it with your own eyes. It's so large, bacteria grow on it.

163.   In the 1930s, Finch Telecommunications Laboratories created a machine that faxed the owner their daily newspaper so they wouldn't have to go out and buy one. It was a great idea at the time, but it failed after too many mechanical failures.

164.   In 1982, Italdesign created the Capsula car. This car's entire cabin could be replaced and switched with a different kind of car. No one took the idea seriously and it has remained a prototype for decades.

165.   More people were killed during WWII, manufacturing V-2 Rockets than were killed by the rockets themselves.

166.   Your DNA is 1/80 billionth of an inch wide.

167. An iPhone user unlocks their device about 80 times daily.

168. Andrew Charalambous constructed his club, Bar Surya, with a kinetic dance floor. When clubbers danced, the energy from their movements were absorbed by the piezoelectric cells of the ground and convert it into electricity, therefore rendering batteries unnecessary. It also saves 60% on energy.

169. To build a Death Star like the one depicted in Star Wars, would cost $852 quadrillion. That's 13,000 times more money than is on Earth.

170. A linguist and a sound engineer tried to find the perfect male voice by listening to dozens of famous actors. They concluded that the perfect voice was a combination of Alan Rickman and Jeremy Irons.

171. In the 1960s, Dome homes were designed to withstand hurricanes and earthquakes. Sadly, the were never mass-produced because people thought they looked silly.

172. There's enough fuel in a full tank of a jumbo jet to drive a normal car around the world four times.

173. Scrooge, Or, Marley's Ghost was a British film made in 1901. It was the first film to have intertitles. An intertitle is an image that is visible at the same time as the title.

174. The 1929 film, Woman in the Moon, was the first film to show a countdown before a launch. And that's not just on film. It was the first film to have a countdown launch anywhere since this was over 30 years before man went to the Moon.

175. The chief translator for the European Parliament is Ioannis Ikonoou. He is fluent in 32 languages.

176. The 1925 film, The Lost World, was the first Hollywood feature film to be shown as an in-flight movie.

177. Nine million British people have never used the Internet.

178. The first photograph that was uploaded to the Internet was in 1989. It was a picture of four women with the words, "Les Horribles Cernettes" above them. The girls were a band that sang about physics. The photograph was uploaded by the Swiss laboratory, CERN.

179. Chemotherapy is a by-product of the mustard gas used in WWI.

180. Manel Torres invented the first spray-on clothing. Within minutes, the clothes will adjust to the wearer's physique.

181. In the Harry Potter series, Shirley Henderson plays the 11-year-old Moaning Myrtle. Henderson was 45 at the time.

182. Scientifically, it's more likely to rain on the weekends. The reason why is because dust and carbon monoxide build up over the week from cars travelling to and from work, which forms clouds. With the reduction in emissions over the weekend, the rain comes.

183. Swearing on the Bible is forbidden according to the Bible.

184. Most people pour juice from a carton with the opening closer to the glass. However, you are far more likely to spill the drink this way. If you pour juice with the opening on top, it will spray down more evenly.

185. If a corporation has an income of over $50,000, it pays a tax rate of 15%. If a corporation has an income of over $18,333,333, it has a tax rate of 35%. Google is worth approximately $107.4 billion. Do you know how much tax they pay? 2.4%. Google use a technique called Double Irish, which involves transferring money overseas. Microsoft and Facebook use a similar technique, which is why they pay less tax than you.

186. Pfizer created an inhalable insulin called Exubera in 2006 so diabetics don't have to inject themselves with an insulin needle. It took 11 years to perfect the technology, which would have changed diabetes sufferers forever. Sadly, the product failed as patient found the inhaler too bulky.

187. Pay By Touch was an idea in 2002 to make payments without cash or cards. Instead, you use your finger. Utilizing biometrics, this technology scans your fingerprints so you don't need to carry cash or cards.   Sadly, this tech never came to be as the CEO, John Rogers, was involved in a scandal and the company went bankrupt in 2007.

188. Duncan MacDougal weighed dying people because he believed that humans lost a small amount of weight upon death as the soul left the body. While conducting his experiments, he abductively reasoned that the human body lost 21.3 grams upon death. He further "proved" his findings by performing the same experiment on a dying dog and noticed that it lost no weight upon death due to the fact that only humans have souls. Unsurprisingly, many scientists found MacDougal's research and findings highly questionable.

189. Michael Persinger claimed he invented a helmet to see God. The device is a modified snowmobile helmet that sends magnetic fields to the wearer's parietal and temporal lobes. 80% of the people who used it said they felt God or a dead loved one was in the room.

190. Albert Bandura wanted to see if children acted out violence if they saw adults acting aggressively. To test this, he made a movie which depicted adults beating up a clown. He then showed the film to kids. When he introduced the kids to a real clown, the children instantly attacked him.

191. Speed dating was invented by a rabbi.

192. Ivanhoe reservoir learned that their water had become contaminated and would become radioactive when exposed to sunlight. So, the LA Department of water covered its surface with 400,000 plastic balls, blocking the sunlight from reaching the water surface.

193. During WWII, many Nazis took methamphetamine to maximize their alertness and endurance.

194. Oscillococcinum is a flu treatment that emphasizes how

efficient it is because it is made of duck liver. However, the duck liver is so diluted in the treatment, you need to consume 10^{380} pills to consume ONE molecule of the duck liver.

195. A Chinese girl went missing when she was 14 and was presumed dead. She was found ten years later living in an Internet café. It turns out that she was so good at the video game, Cross Fire, other gamers paid to watch her play.

196. Y-chromosome Adam is the name that geneticists call the oldest male man that humanity descended from. He lived approximately 208,000 years ago and he would be you 8,317th-great-grandfather.

197. During WWII, the Nazis killed six million Jews. During the same war, the Japanese killed at least seven million Chinese.

198. All the numbers on a roulette wheel add up to 666.

199. In 1900, all the world's mathematical knowledge could be written in about 80 books. Nowadays, it takes up over 100,000 books.

200. In the Middle Ages, beer was consumed more than water.

201. When you first logged onto iTunes, there was a huge document that you had to agree to before you could set up your account. If you read that document (which nobody ever does,) you have agreed not use Apple products to create nuclear weapons.

202. Mail-order marriages in the US are less likely to end in divorce than regular marriages.

203. 33% of all divorces in the US in 2011 involved Facebook.

204. The first thing ever bought and sold on the Internet was a bag of marijuana in 1971.

205. The movie, TRON, didn't win an Oscar for its groundbreaking special effects because the academy claimed the movie "cheated" because it used computers.

206. The Rubik's cube has 43,252,003,274,489,856,000 combinations. If you could solve every combination in one second, it would take over three million times the age of the universe to solve them all.

207. Antarctica is the only continent without a time zone.

208. The ice sheet of Antarctica has existed for over 40 million years.

209. There are 300 lakes beneath Antarctica that can't freeze because they are too near the Earth's core.

210. Every time you smell a violet, you're smelling it for the first time. A violet's scent comes from compounds called ionones that work by shutting off your scent receptors, forcing you to immediately forget the smell.

211. Morgan Robertson wrote a book called Futility which was about the sinking of the supposedly unsinkable ship, the Titan. In the book, the Titan crashed into an iceberg 400 miles from Newfoundland at 25 knots. The Titanic crashed into an iceberg 400 miles from Newfoundland at 22.5 knots. Robertson's book was written 14 years before the Titanic was built.

212. James Lewis was adopted as a baby. He married a woman called Linda, divorced her, then married a woman called Betty who had a son called James Alan.
    Years later, he tracked down his twin brother, James Springer. Springer also married a woman called Linda, divorced her, married another woman called Betty and had a son called James Alan.

213. Project Stargate was a 20-year-long government program created in 1978 and employed 22 full-time "psychics." The division was formed after Command heard rumors that Soviets had psychics working for them.

214. Mathematicians have calculated pi to 12.1 trillion digits. If this was written down, it would reach approximately 186 million miles. That's twice the distance between the Earth and

the Sun.

215. 205 billion emails are sent per day.

216. There is no computer that can calculate every move in chess... and there never will be. The amount of moves in chess are 1 followed by 120 zeroes. It's called the Shannon number. There are far more moves in chess than there are atoms in the universe. There are over 300 billion possible combinations in the first four moves in a game of chess. There are 170 septillion possibilities in just the first ten moves. That's 170,000,000,000,000,000,000,000,000 possible moves.

217. The Coco de Mer palm tree has the world's largest fruit, weighing 92lbs. Even the seeds weigh 37lbs.

218. The largest prime number found is $2^{57,885,161} - 1$. If you wrote this number down, it would be 23 miles long.

219. Richard Buckminster Fuller was an architect who developed the geodesic dome. He also wrote a book for 66 years about his life. If his book was stacked, it would stand 1,400ft tall. That's 150ft higher than the Empire State Building.

220. As the Titanic was about to set sail, the ship's second officer, David Blair, was replaced with Charles Lightoller. However, Blair forgot to give Lightoller the key for the locker that contained the binoculars. If Lightoller had the binoculars, he would've easily seen the iceberg that the Titanic crashed into.

221. During WWII, a special force of Jewish soldiers hunted down and killed hundreds of former Nazis. They called themselves The Avengers.

222. The fire hydrant was patented in 1801 by Frederick Graff. It wasn't invented until later because the Patent Office was burned down, destroying all the records.

223. When the Titanic sunk, one newspaper said, "Passengers safely moved and steamer Titanic taken in tow."

224. In The Lord of the Rings story, the hobbits walk 1,779 miles.

225. A real estate developer calculated that the construction of Hogwarts building from the Harry Potter series would require 414,000sq ft. That's nearly eight times the size of the White house.

A building would cost $204,102,000. That's nearly double the budget of the first Harry Potter film.

226. At Wendy's, the chicken Caesar salad is 780 calories with 51g of fat. By comparison, the pretzel bacon cheeseburger is 680 calories and has 36g of fat.

227. Bananas have more trade regulations than AK-47s.

228. Lego heads have a hole so a child will be able to breathe if they swallowed it.

229. Most doorknobs are made from brass because the material disinfects itself and kills 99% of the germs on it within two hours.

230. An olive tree can live for 1,500 years.

231. Oliver "Porky" Bickar flew a hundred tires into an Alaskan volcano called Mt. Edgecumb and then set them on fire so everyone in the area would think the volcano was going to erupt. Not only that, he did this on April Fool's Day, knowing that everyone would make emergency phone calls and nobody would believe them.

What a guy.

232. On April Fool's Day of 2007, Google sent an email to its employees that a python was loose in the building. It wasn't a prank.

233. Sarcasm used to confuse people when it was written down because readers couldn't tell when the writer was being sarcastic. As a result, a sarcastic punctuation mark was strongly considered in the 1580s. It was called the SarcMark.

234. "Snooze alarms" is an anagram of "Alas no more z's."

235.   The first car, the Model T, had a 20-horsepower engine. That is the same as a modern riding lawnmower.

236.   John Brunner wrote the book, Stand on Zanzibar, in 1968. It takes place in 2010 and the president is a black man called Obomi.

237.   The Nobel Peace prize depicts three naked men.

238.   Peanuts are one of the ingredients of dynamite.

239.   Only three English words begin with "dw" – dwarf, dwelling, and dwindle.

240.   Adidas and Puma were founded by brothers. They were also Nazis.

241.   Chocolate chip cookies were created by accident when the chocolate in the cookie didn't melt properly. The cookies inventor, Ruth Wakefield, made $1 from her invention.

242.   The bulletproof vest was invented by a pizza delivery guy after he got shot twice while on the job.

243.   The Cathode Ray Tube Amusement Device was the first attempt at creating a video game. It was built in the 1940s and was similar to a radar.

244.   A group of officers is called a mess.

245.   "J" is the only letter that is absent from the Periodic Table.

246.   "Underground" is the only English word that begins and ends with "und."

247.   "Dreamt" is the only English word that ends with "mt."

248.   "Strengths" is the longest word in the English language that has one syllable.

249.   There are 293 ways to make change for $1.

250.   When you see lightning, it has already struck the ground twice. It happens so fast, there's no way you can see it strike the first time.

251.   Thumb hard drives can hold 256 gigabytes. That's the same as 213,000 floppy disks. If you lay that many floppy disks end to end, it would be nearly 18 miles long.

252.   Until gas masks were invented for war, soldiers tied urine-soaked socks onto their faces. The ammonia from the urine combatted the gas.

253.   Mike Tyson has adored pigeons since he was a child. After a bully killed Tyson's pet pigeon in front of him, Tyson decided to take up boxing. That's right. Tyson became a world boxing champion at 19... because of a pigeon.

254.   There's $80.9 trillion on Earth. If it was divided equally, each person would get just over $11,000. However, that is only if the money existed in physical form. 92% of the money on Earth only exists digitally.

255.   A group of Native Americans called Tarahumara can run 200 miles a day barefoot through rocky terrain. They will hunt animals and will never give up chasing their prey unless they collapse from exhaustion. They will run for a hundred miles while kicking a ball just for fun.

256.   Louis Cyr may have been the strongest man to ever live. He could lift a 215lb barbell with one hand. He could carry 2,371lbs (slightly over a ton) on his back.

257.   50% of human DNA is identical to cabbage. Seriously.

258.   Philadelphia physician, Arthur Lintgen, can recognize classic musical composition within seconds by just looking at the grooves of a phonograph. Just by touching the grooves, he can tell you the name of the music, the composer, the orchestra, and the conductor.

259.   The world debt is $199 trillion. That's over double the amount of money that exists.

260. An ice cyclone called a brinicle can form underwater. If it touches any living thing (usually starfish,) they will freeze to death within seconds. It has gained the nickname "the ice finger of death."

261. You can oxygenate water to make it breathable. This was shown in the film, The Abyss.

262. If you drop a suspended slinky from one end, only the top will fall. Until the top impacts the bottom, the bottom part hangs motionless in the air. For one second, a slinky seems to defy the laws of gravity.

263. The steering wheel was invented eight years after the car.

264. Aerogel provides 39 times more insulation than the best fiberglass insulation. It is lightest material ever created. It is 1/6th the density of air and can balance perfectly on a flower, even if it's the size of a can of Coke.

265. Susan Bennett is the voice of Siri. Her voice was chosen without her permission. She never auditioned and didn't know she was the voice of Siri until the day the program debuted.

266. Ancient Romans celebrated Saturnalia; a festival where masters and slaves swapped places.

267. There is a form of matter called supercritical fluid. It is part-gas and part-liquid. Nowadays, its most commonly used to make decaffeinated coffee taste better.

268. A superfluid is a unique type of liquid that can leak through solid matter. If it was put into a sealed jar, the superfluid would pass through it. Superfluid is created when liquid helium's temperature is dropped to -271 degrees Celsius (two degrees above absolute zero.)

269. Gallium is a liquid metal (like mercury) that melts at room temperature. It also melts aluminum if it encounters the metal.

270. It takes 400 cacao beans to make 1lb of chocolate.

271.   A heat-proof plastic called Starlite was invented in 1990. An egg was put inside the plastic and then burned with a blowtorch at 1,200 degrees Celsius. When the plastic was peeled open, the egg was completely uncooked.

Simulations have been done on Starlite that show it would survive an atomic blast.

It was invented by a hairdresser called Maurice Ward. He never told anyone how to make it and he died in 2011. No one knows how to duplicate his work.

272.   Hamburgers from most fast-food restaurants have fake grill marks imprinted on them.

273.   Mountain Dew contains brominated vegetable oil (BVO.) Consuming too much BVO can lead to memory loss and nerve disorders.

274.   If you counted one number per second eight hours a day, five days a week, 50 weeks a year, it would take four years to count to ten million. If you counted one number per second, it would take 32 years to count to a billion. However, this is impossible as larger numbers take more than a second to pronounce. Also, you may need to eat or sleep at some point.

275.   A man called Armand Hammer coincidentally became a member of the board of directors for Arm & Hammer.

276.   There is a plant that can produce tomatoes and potatoes. It is known as the "Ketchup 'n' Fries" plant.

277.   Scientists have recently created synthetic DNA Hydrogel; a material that can remember its shape. You can twist it to make a very specific shape (like your name) and scrunch it up, but it will revert to the shape of your name if you place it in water.

278.   Sodium acetate can only freeze after it's been heated.

279.   Maria Carey's legs are insured for $1 billion.

280.   Apples, peaches, and raspberries are all genetically linked to the rose flower.

281. Plutonium costs $40,000 per gram.

282. 70% of sent emails are spam.

283. There is an online service called Invisible Girlfriend. For a payment, this package will send you a hundred texts, ten voicemails, and a handwritten note from your non-existent partner.

284. There's a website called the somethingstore.com If you send the site $10, they will send you a completely random object e.g. headphones, scarf, hat, cheese knife, sunglasses, bath robe, Kindle Fire, etc.

285. In 1631, a huge reprint of the Bible was recalled and burnt because there was a typo that stated, "Thou shalt commit adultery."

286. In 2014, a completely new form of matter called disordered hyperuniformity was discovered in the eye of a chicken.

287. Mt. Everest is 8,848 meters (29,035ft.) To give you an idea of how high this is, that's 2,400 meters higher than airplanes usually fly. That's ten times higher than Burj Khalifa, which is the tallest building in the world.

288. The screwdriver was invented 300 years after the screw.

289. Although humanity have been using fire for approximately 10,000 years, matches didn't exist until 1826.

290. Bread was created in 29000 BC. Sliced bread wasn't created until 1928.

291. Tennis for Two is considered to be the first official video game. It was created by William Higinbotham on October 18th 1958. It was built on an oscilloscope. Players used two aluminium controllers to play the game.

292. Play-doh was invented to remove soot stains on wallpaper. Play-doh was originally called Kutol Rainbow Modelling

Compound.

293.   Scientists have created a liquid magnet called Ferrofluid.

294.   Flowers grow faster when exposed to relaxing music.

295.   In 1979, Elvita Adams jumped from the 86th floor of the Empire State Building in an attempted suicide, only to be blown into the 85th floor by a gust of wind. Her only injury was a broken hip.

296.   Although the flu virus can only live on your skin for five minutes, it can survive on paper currency for 17 days.

297.   In May 2011, two Muslims were removed from an airplane because passengers felt uncomfortable with them onboard. The men were on their way to attend a conference for Muslims that have suffered from prejudice.

298.   Sulfur hexafluoride is the densest gas in the universe. It's so dense, solid objects can float on it. It's known as the "cousin" to helium.
       If helium is inhaled, it will make a person's voice sound high-pitched. If sulfur hexafluoride is inhaled, it will make a person's voice so deep, it will make him or her sound like Darth Vader.

299.   A thimethylsilanol coating has been created that makes certain materials impossible to get wet... even when they are underwater. It has been proven to be 100% successful against sand.

300.   Scientists from Rice University have recently created spray-on batteries. The technology is still in its infancy, but it's still a monumental achievement.

301.   The PU elastomer is a new polymer material that can heal itself. If it's cut in half, it will reconnect if the pieces are put back together. It has the nickname "terminator polymer" due to its similarity to the T-1000 robot from the film, Terminator 2: Judgment Day.

302.   In early 2016, when America Republican primary voters

were asked if the US should pre-emptively bomb Agrabah, 40% said yes. Agrabah is the fictional country from the Disney film, Aladdin.

303.   Soccer means "association."

304.   98% of Antarctica is made of ice. Most of the ice is one mile thick.

305.   Eating 20 apple cores in a row can be lethal due to high levels of cyanide.

306.   In 2012, Walmart's best-selling product was the banana.

307.   Although blackcurrant is extremely popular in most countries, it's banned throughout most of the United States.

308.   Only 5% of Twitter users have more than a hundred followers.

309.   Spencer Gore was the first Wimbledon tennis champion. He said "lawn tennis is a bit boring. It will never catch on."

310.   The cleaning product, Cillit Bang, is surprisingly effective against plutonium stains.

311.   If you crack an egg 60ft underwater, it will stay together.

312.   Caroyln Davidson designed the Nike logo in 1971. She was paid $35 for her services.

313.   In the UK, the most common profession that a criminal applies for after they leave prison is teaching.

314.   Doodle boards like Magna Doodle are a big hit with kids because it allows them to draw and erase pictures endlessly.
       However, the "toy" was invented in 1974 for board rooms and business meetings. The creators, Pilot Pen, advertised it as a "dustless chalkboard."
       Although it never took off for adults, it became a major success with kids.

315. The word "okay" comes from the Latin "Omnis Korrecta," which means "all correct."

316. According to the WWF, the Earth has lost 40% of its wildlife in the last 40 years.

317. It would take seven hours of walking to burn off a Super-Sized Coke, French fries, and a Big Mac.

318. Diana Ross sang Ain't No Mountain High Enough. Her ex-husband died in a mountain climbing accident.

319. A tension spring stabilizes equipment on board ships during WWII. In 1943, Richard James knocked over a bunch of springs and noticed how they kept flipping over and over. James thought he could sell the bouncing springs as a children's toy. In 1945, he released his product, which became an instant success. It is known as the Slinky.

320. Did you ever wonder why people put "x" at the end of a text to represent a kiss?
    Well, during the Middle Ages, most people were illiterate and signed documents with an "x" and then kissed it for sincerity.

321. Mouthing the word "colorful" looks the same as "I love you."

322. Every year, rugs kill 3,800 people, lawnmowers kill 90 people, stairs, kill 12,000, and window blind cords kill seven.

323. In March 2014, a British sniper station in Afghanistan killed six insurgents with one bullet. He shot a suicide bomber, which trigger his device, killing five other terrorists.

324. Gordon Ramsay left one of his first restaurant jobs because he couldn't put up with "the rages, the bullying, and violence" from the chef.

325. The first time someone tried to publish the secrets of the Freemasons, he was kidnapped and murdered.

326. The most children born to one woman is 69. She had 16 twins, seven triplets, and four quadruplets.

327.   Google was supposed to be called "Googol" but the founder didn't know how to spell it.

328.   A man from Minnesota used a 3D printer and an Arduino microcontroller to build a castle. It was 3 x 5 meters big and it was made of concrete.

329.   Duct tape was invented by the Johnson and Johnson Company to seal ammunition cases during World War II.

330.   Musician, Barry Manilow, is famous for his song, I Write the Songs. He didn't write it.

331.   "Silly" used to be mean "prosperous." It wasn't until the 1570s that it meant "foolish and lacking in reason." Speaking of silly...

332.   Silly putty was created as a substitute for rubber during World War II. Rubber was limited but necessary for soldiers' boots, gas masks, and tires.

333.   Until the 14th century, "artificial" meant "highly skilled."

334.   "Companion" is derived from a Latin word which means "someone with whom you share bread."

335.   The African Bloodwood trees are so-called because they have red sap, which gives the impression that the trees are bleeding.

336.   "A decimal point" is an anagram of "I'm a dot in place."

337.   The word "Lucifer" in the Bible refers to the fall of Babylon, not Satan.

338.   Humans have 1-4% Neanderthal DNA. This means that our homo sapien ancestors mated with Neanderthals at some point.

339.   Diamonds cost up to $33,000 per carat.

340. Iguanas and chameleons can be venomous.

341. Bears, gophers, and camels are prone to osteoporosis if they are kept in captivity.

342. The word "hazard" is an Old French word meaning "an unfortunate throw of dice." It used to refer to gambling with one's life.

343. No educated person believed the Earth was flat since 500 BC.

344. Toshuyuki Takahashi can press a controller button 16 times in one second. This is the world record.

345. In 1900, 22% of cars were power by gasoline, 38% by electricity, and 40% by steam.

346. The chainsaw was invented for surgery.

347. "Disaster" comes from the Italian word "disastrato," which means "born under an ill star."

348. Up until a century ago, wristwatches were seen as a dainty, feminine fad. The New York Times said that wristwatches were "been looked upon by Americans as more or less of a joke" and "a silly ass fad."
    Wristwatches didn't become popular until they were adopted by the military.

349. One study showed that 12 reported deaths have been linked to balloons between 2010 to 2012.

350. Earl Sampson is a black man from Florida who has been arrested 62 times in the same convenience store because he looked suspicious.
    He works there.

351. Automatic vehicles were created to make driving easier for women as the manufacturers believed that they couldn't drive manual cars.

352. Candy floss was co-created by a dentist.

353. The word "awful" used to mean the opposite of what it means today. "Awful" meant "awe-inspiring" or "full of awe." It wasn't until 1809 that it took on the same meaning as the Old English word "egefull," which means "very bad."

354. Annette Kellerman was the first woman to wear a one-piece bathing suit in 1907. She was arrested for "indecent exposure."

355. The can opener was invented 45 years after the can.

356. 99% of people backspace their entire password when they mess up one letter.

357. There's a beer brewed from bananas in Africa.

358. Statistically, a man cries six times a year. A woman cries 30-64 times per year.

359. In March 2016, James and Bob Stocklas bought tickets for the Powerball Jackpot. James won the $291.4 million dollars. His brother, Bob, won $7. Some sources say that Bob may or may not have bought a sandwich with his winnings.

360. Long before trees were common, the planet was covered with 24ft tall mushrooms.

361. The word "idiot" used to mean "anyone who wasn't a politician."

362. "Mortgage" originally meant "death contract."

363. The most overdue library book ever was returned 288 years late.

364. There are more living organisms in a teaspoonful of soil than there are people on Earth.

365. "School" originally meant "free time."

366.   In British Columbia, doctors are not allowed to talk about hockey during surgery.

367.   A Cleveland Browns fan requested six Cleveland Browns pallbearers at his funeral so "the Browns could let him down one last time."

368.   33% of all the arable land on Earth has been lost in the last 40 years.

369.   8.7% of Facebook users are fake.

370.   "The Morse code" is an anagram of "here comes dots."

371.   When the Nazis held its first book burnings, one of the works destroyed was an 1821 play by Heinrich Heine, which contained the phrase, "Where they burn books, they will also in the end, burn people."

372.   During WWII, the Soviets built a flying tank.

373.   You know how you can create fire with a magnifying glass?
         Well, did you know that trick also works with a block of ice? That's right. You can make fire... from ice.
         Survivalists in the cold will try to keep warm by finding the clearest piece of ice they can find, shaping it into a circular disc and then smoothing out the surface. Then they have to get some kindling and angle the ice between the Sun and the kindling. The ice will act like a magnifying glass and ignite the kindling with the focused sunlight.
         You can find videos on YouTube of a man called Tim Jones demonstrating this amazing feat.

374.   Between 1971-1986, the red M&M was discontinued as people believed the dye in the chocolate (FD&C red No.2) caused cancer.

375.   It's possible to open a can without a can-opener. And I know what you're thinking. You just smash it against a rock, right? You could do that but you run the risk of losing the food inside the can.

In the absence of a can-opener, the best thing to do is to turn the can upside down and rub it against a flat piece of concrete for a minute.

After that, all you have to do is squeeze the can and the lid will pop off.

376.   M&M's were created in 1941 so army soldiers could eat chocolate without it melting in their hands.

377.   27,000 trees are cut down every day for toilet paper.

378.   Refined sugar is more addictive than cocaine.

379.   Crayons can be used as a substitute for candles. They can last up to 30 minutes.

380.   Ramon Artagaveytia's ship sunk in 1871, which left him with a severe phobia of sailing. After over 40 years, he finally decided to sail again in 1912. He died while on the Titanic.

381.   Pop, Goes the Weasel is a nursery rhyme that is about pawning your clothes when you have no money left. "Pop" is a Cockney slang, which means "to sell something at a pawn shop." A "weasel" was a common term for a "coat" in Britain in the 19th century.

382.   80% of all the machinery in a car is recyclable.

383.   Colin Furze invented shoes that become magnetized to metal. The shoes are so magnetic, he can hang upside-down from a metal ceiling while wearing them. They are called Magneto Shoes.

384.   Paper can be recycled six times.

385.   The inventor of Vaseline ate a spoonful of it daily.

386.   Terror and horror are two different feelings. Terror is the feeling that occurs before a scary experience. Horror is what a person feels after a scary experience.

387. There is a Santa Claus University that teaches professional Santa Clauses about toys, voices, poses, etc. A professional Santa can make up to $100,000 per year.

388. Platinum cost $1,300 per ounce.

389. All evidence shows that writing was only invented three times in history – in the Middle East, China, and Central America. All other alphabets and writing systems were derived or inspired from another language.

390. It would take ten years to view all the photos shared on Snapchat in the last hour.

391. In 2009, a Google programmer made a typo and accidentally flagged every site on the Internet as dangerous.

392. Now that most computers use touchpads, mousepads seem obsolete. However, a mousepad is incredibly advanced. Every passing second, a mousepad takes 1,500 pictures of the surface underneath it and then sends the photos to the mouse's optical navigation engine, which processes them to calculate how it is moving.

393. According to polls done on Western women, the most attractive male names are Ryan, Jack, and James. The least attractive male names were polled as Thomas, Peter, and George. According to polls done on Western men, the most attractive female names are Sophie, Rachel, and Olivia. The least attractive female names were polled as Jane, Ann, and Helen.

394. Soccer players run about 9.5 miles in a single match.

395. A gymnasium dumbbell has 362 times more bacteria than the average toilet.

396. Carrie Swidecki played Just Dance for 138 hours straight, which is the world record.

397. Every drop of ink from a printer is heated and vaporized, which creates a bubble that explodes and launches the ink onto

the page at 30 miles per hour. This happens 36,000 times per second, through a nozzle less than the width of a human hair.

398.   The creator of the Pringles packaging had his ashes stored in a Pringle can after he died.

399.   The bird on the Twitter icon is called Larry.

400.   The brain of a monkey and sheep grow exponentially while in the womb. Most of the smartest animals such as pigs and humans have their brains grow rapidly shortly after birth.

401.   Africa is the only continent to have land on all four hemispheres.

402.   There are 16 African countries with higher vaccination rates than the US.

403.   Google handles over two trillion searches per year. That's 27 searches for every person in the world.

404.   153,000 people die every day. Remember this fact on your birthday.

405.   Human beings are the only animals that like spicy food.

406.   Victor Marx is the fastest disarmer in the world. He can disarm someone pointing a gun directly against his forehead in a fraction of a second. He can even disarm several attackers simultaneously.

407.   Scientists have identified 510 DNA codes that have been lost due to evolution.

408.   Antarctica has one ATM.

409.   A signal light in a nuclear power station was programmed to indicate when the computer had a sent a signal to close a valve. However, the light was NOT designed to confirm when the valve was actually closed. So, when the computer sent a signal to shut the valve and it didn't work, nobody could tell that anything was wrong. As a result, the reactor overheated

and caused the nuclear disaster known as the Three Mile Island accident.

410.   Isao Machii is a samurai that can split a bullet travelling at 217mph in two with his sword.

411.   Most people lose consciousness once they go higher than 15,000ft.

412.   In 2011, a Netherlands study showed that people who are good at holding in their pee also have good long-term money management skills.

413.   Vikings used to baptize children with beer.

414.   A 19-year-old Brit changed his name to Captain Fantastic Faster Than Superman Spiderman Batman Wolverine Hulk and The Flash Combined. His grandmother is no longer speaking to him.

415.   Russians used to believe that Jews consumed a secret vegetable to stop them from suffering from alcoholism.

416.   The earlier you develop language skills as a baby, the more likely you will become a heavy drinker later in life.

417.   A person diving into water without equipment usually gets 60ft before they black out. The world record is 282ft.

418.   The 1% richest people on Earth own 48% of the world's wealth.

419.   By 1850, 20% of US wealth was made up of slaves.

420.   The taller someone is, the more likely they will get cancer.

421.   Google has a version of their website translated into Klingon; the fictional language from Star Trek.

422.   Aerial Manx is an Australian acrobat who can do multiple backflips with a sword down his throat.

423.   Travis Tomasie can load a gun faster than anyone. He can reload his gun in half a second, even if he doesn't have a clip in his hand.

424.   Movie trailers used to play after films.

425.   In 1907, a book called Friday the Thirteenth, was published. This novel inspired the idea that Friday the 13th is cursed. As a result, the American economy loses $900 million on that day because workers will call in sick because they are worried that something bad will happen if they venture outside. Even the stock market noticeably suffers and drops by about 0.2% on this day. Since there were three Friday the 13th's in 2015, the American economy lost approximately $2.7 billion in three days.

426.   People in the Western world (especially European males) have grown 4-5 inches over the last century. Weirdly, the average height of Africans has shrunk by about the same amount in the same amount of time.

427.   Gold has been found on eucalyptus trees.

428.   The world's largest gold bar weighs 551lbs.

429.   It takes 50 glasses of water to grow the oranges to make one glass of orange juice.

430.   Tom Sietas can hold his breath for 22 minutes and 22 seconds, which is the world record.

431.   It takes 2,900 gallons of water to make a single pair of jeans.

432.   Google Earth's database is over 20 petabytes. That's 20 million gigabytes.

433.   The first cave painters were women.

434.   6% of people's dreams are classified as nightmares.

435. A ten-year-old boy accidentally created a new molecule in 2012 in a science class called Tetranitratoxycarbon.

436. Vantablack is the darkest material in the world. It absorbs 99.965% of radiation in the visible spectrum. It is so dark, people who look at it say it makes them feel "uneasy."

437. It costs $8,876 per year to own and maintain an average car in the US. That's $443,800 over a period of 50 years.

438. After the Titanic sunk, the families of the band members onboard were billed for the cost of their uniforms.

439. When Kim Kardashian was on Myspace, she never had more than a thousand followers. She now has 45 million followers on Twitter.

440. There are 30 million Facebook accounts of people who have died.

441. The youngest professional gamer is Victor De Leon III. He was seven years old when he was signed by Major League Gaming as a professional video gamer. He started playing when he was two and entered professional competitions when he was five. He likes to be known as Lil Poison.

442. The song, Jingle Bells, was created for Thanksgiving.

443. Two actors have died playing Judas Iscariot in live Biblical productions by accidentally hanging themselves during their suicide scene.

444. "The eyes" is an anagram of "they see."

445. When a human being is blindfolded, it is impossible for them to walk in a straight line. Try it if you don't believe me.

446. Holocaust denial is illegal in 17 countries.

447. Thomas Earl was fired, mauled by a bear, and shot by the police…on the same day. He might have the world record for having the Worst Day Ever.

448.   The world's strongest superglue originated from a bug called caulobacter crescentus.

449.   The glass sponge deserves its name. Although most sponges are made of spongin, the glass sponge is composed of silica that is so thick, its bones are literally made of glass.

450.   In 1972, a pocket of uranium in Africa was discovered that had undergone self-sustaining nuclear fission for hundreds of thousands of years, making it the only naturally formed nuclear reactor.

451.   The 2015 movie, Noah, which revolves around the Biblical Flood, was delayed for a year due to flooding.

452.   The Radiation symbol was created in 1946.

453.   Statistically, atheists are the most likely people to know details about other religions.

454.   Soliris is the most expensive medical drug in the world, costing $5,000 for 30ml. It cost $400,000 to be treated with it for a year.

455.   Katy Perry's mother dated Jimi Hendrix.

456.   Gold costs $40 per gram.

457.   Daily shampooing wasn't considered the norm until the 1970s.

458.   "&" and "and" mean different things in movie credits. If two writers' names are joined with "&," that means they worked together. If two writers' names are written with the word, "and," it means they worked on the movie at different times.

459.   Brandenn Bremmer was a born genius. He had an IQ of 178 and could read books when he was only 18 months old. Bremmer could play the piano when he was three and started

college when he was 11. He committed suicide at 14 with no signs of depression and he didn't leave a suicide note.

460.   The price of cocaine has gone down by 51% since 1990.

461.   "Election results" is an anagram of "lies let's recount."

462.   The Dutch East India Company was the richest company in history. In its prime, it was worth $7.4 trillion.

463.   A Swedish man received disability benefits due to his heavy metal addiction. He went to 300 concerts a year, which left him unable to hold down a job.

464.   The most expensive material on Earth is anti-matter. It cost $62.5 trillion... per gram. That's almost four times the national debt of America. It's used for the Large Hadron Collider in Switzerland to recreate the first moments of the Big Bang.

465.   An average swimming pool loses 1,000 gallons of water each month from evaporation.

466.   Living next to a nuclear plant for a year would give you 100 times less radiation than eating a bag of crisps every day for a year.

467.   The CIA burn classified documents to heat their water.

468.   When the game, Twister was introduced in 1966, it was denounced by critics as "sex in a box."

469.   A recycled can will be back on a grocery store shelf within 60 days.

470.   The tallest man was Robert Wadlow. He was 8ft 11 and was still growing when he died in 1940 at the age of 22. Also, he was a Freemason.

471.   The Giant Water Lilly is 10ft across and can easily support the weight of a small child.

472.   The carnivorous plant, the Nepenthaceae rajah can eat frogs,

birds, and rats.

473. Talin is the sweetest substance in the world. It is 3,250 times sweeter than sugar.

474. Gennaro Pelliccia tastes every single batch of coffee beans for Costa Coffee. He has trained himself to distinguish between thousands of different flavors. He has insured his tongue for $14 million.

475. 44% of people on Twitter have never tweeted.

476. Lucia Zarate was the lightest adult in recorded history. When she died at 17, she was 2ft 2 and weighed 4lbs.

477. The battery of an Apple MacBook is bulletproof.

478. Over 80,000 people graduated from McDonald's hamburger university and received a bachelor's degree in Hamburgerology.

479. The song, Amazing Grace was written by a slave ship captain.

480. Alan Knight pretended to be in a coma for two years to avoid going to court after he was caught stealing £45,000.

481. Enya is one of the world's best-selling artists and sold over 100 million albums. She has never gone on tour.

482. The police were unable to locate a serial killer called Rodney Alcala until he appeared as a contestant on The Dating Game. He murdered up to 130 people.

483. Donald Trump cheated on his first wife in a church.

484. Noclue is the fastest rapper in the world. He can say 723 syllables in 51.27 seconds. That's 14.1 syllables per second.

485. During a car crash, 40% of drivers don't hit the brakes.

486.   99% of your DNA is identical to every human being on Earth. This means that you have 99% of the same DNA as Tom Cruise and Abraham Lincoln. And Hitler.

487.   Audrey Marie Hilley killed her husband and then faked her death. She then returned to a "normal" life as her fake twin sister. She was caught and died soon after from a heart attack.

488.   "Slot machines" is an anagram of "cash lost in me."

489.   5% of soccer injuries are caused by celebrating goals.

490.   When the first train was built, people didn't want to ride it because they genuinely believed that travelling over 50mph would rip their faces off and "cause a woman's uterus to fly out of her body."
    This has probably never happened.

491.   Ma Xiangang has the highest tolerance to electricity known to man. His resistance to electric shocks is seven or eight times higher than an average human.

492.   A Bonsai tree planted in 1626 survived the atomic explosion in Hiroshima. Nowadays, it resides in a US museum.

493.   Wang "Banana" Jiao is the most well-paid gamer in the world. He was last reported to have $1,192,049.89 in prize-money from winning video game tournaments.

494.   To sell tomatoes and apples, the fruits are genetically altered to look bigger, redder, and shinier. Ironically, this drastically changes their tastes. Until 70 years ago, tomatoes always tasted sweet. Nowadays, it's almost impossible to eat a real tomato. Originally, apples could taste like roses, strawberries, popcorn, anise, etc.

495.   Icebergs weigh about 20 million tons.

496.   Clement Wragge was the first meteorologist to give human names to hurricanes and cyclones. Originally, he named them after politicians because they were "causing great distress" and "wandered imlessly."

497. The only 15-letter word that can be spelt without repeating a letter is "uncopyrightable."

498. In 1567, the man with the world's longest beard died when he tripped over it.

499. The average family of four loses 60 socks a year.

500. "The quick brown fox jumps over a lazy dog." is the shortest sentence in the English language that uses every letter in the alphabet.

501. Most new cars have their engine noises amplified with speakers, to give the illusion the engine is more powerful than it is. In reality, modern engines are almost silent.

502. The word "typewriter" can be written with just the top keys of a keyboard.

503. Forest fires move faster uphill than downhill.

504. Apple earns $300,000 per minute.

505. 95% of all data is stored on paper. Most of it will never be looked at again.

506. Recycling one glass jar saves enough energy to watch a television for three hours.

507. In 892 AD, Sigurd the Mighty beheaded a man and then tied his head to his horse's saddle. While riding, a tooth of the decapitated head grazed Sigurd's foot, causing him to die of an infection.
    This means that Sigurd is one of the few people in history to be killed by a decapitated head.

508. More Monopoly money is printed annually than real money.

509. Men are six times more likely to be struck by lightning.

510. A toilet uses six liters of clean water when it is flushed.

511.   The largest snowflake ever found was 15 inches across.

512.   Jurassic Park, Pulp Fiction, Forrest Gump, and The Shawshank Redemption are considered to be the greatest and most influential films of all time. They all came out in October in 1994.

513.   Jose Ayala can channel electricity through his body. With this ability, he can hold an electric wire in his left hand and channel electric current through his body to burn a piece of paper in his right hand. He can do this and not be effected by the electrical current whatsoever.

514.   Viruses can catch viruses.

515.   It took 73 years to find the wreckage of the Titanic.

516.   As of October 2015, Google has acquired 184 companies including Motorola and YouTube. Google spent over $28 billion on these acquisitions.

517.   Jehovah's Witnesses don't celebrate birthdays because the only two accounts of birthdays in the Bible ended in murder.

518.   In 2013, a girl survived Asiana's plane crash. She was then killed by a rescue truck.

519.   The world's first recorded labor strike was held on the site of a pyramid.

520.   Some earthquakes are so powerful, they can permanently shorten the length of Earth's day because their power can alter the spin of Earth's axis.

521.   Even though the Hindenburg blimp had seven million cubic feet of flammable hydrogen gas, it had a smoking room.

522.   A recent poll showed that 9% of Americans fear zombies despite the fact they don't exist.

523.   In 2015, the head of the CIA had his email account hacked by

a teenager.

524. A film about the Titanic was released 29 days after the ship sank. It starred one of the survivors.

525. It's possible to inflate a balloon with your ears.

526. A diabetic's urine can be turned into whiskey because of the high sugar content.

527. The fastest street-legal car is the Bugatti Veyron Super sport, which can travel 267mph.

528. The American military have a 26-page manual on baking brownies and oatmeal cookies.

529. Bananas are mildly radioactive.

530. There's high-speed Internet on Mt. Everest.

531. The 100 richest people in the world earned enough money in 2012 to end poverty four times.

532. During the Middle Ages, castration was used as a cure for a hernia.

533. The Japanese who survived the Titanic were called cowards because they didn't die with the other passengers.

534. Eskimos use refrigerators to stop their food from freezing.

535. You are more likely to die in the bathtub than from terrorism.

536. Cheese is the most commonly stolen food in the world.

537. Nowadays, trees are usually blown up because chopping them down is dangerous.

538. Before the eraser was invented, bread was used to remove pencil marks.

539. The Richter Scale was invented by Charles Richter. He was a nudist.

540. You can be sentenced to jail for make threats entirely in emoji.

541. Studies show that if a person plays video games regularly before they go to bed, it is more likely they will experience lucid dreaming. Lucid dreaming is the ability to control your actions in a dream.

542. It was so cold in February 2015 at Niagara Falls, the entire waterfall froze.

543. A man was arrested for being naked in his own house in Springfield, Virginia.

544. The Inca's measurement of time was based on how long it took to boil a potato.

545. The Nazis considered Native Americans as part of the Aryan race.

546. An Anti-Piracy Ad was fined for pirating music without permission.

547. Robert Lane named his sons, Winner and Loser. Winner became a criminal. Loser became a detective.

548. The last thing that grammarian, Dominque Bouhours said was, "I am about to – or I am going to – die; either expression is correct."

549. During WWII, a ship evaded the Japanese for eight days by disguising itself as an island. The crew covered the whole ship with trees and painted certain parts so they resembled rocks.

550. A comedian called Scott Rogowsky created fake book covers and read them on a subway to see how people reacted to them. Some of the books were titled Mein Kampf for Kids, Human Taxidermy: A Beginner's Guide, and If I Did It, How I Would Have Done 9/11 by George W. Bush.

551.   An American nuclear submarine sank in deep water in 1968. Its nuclear reactor and nuclear weapons have never been retrieved.

552.   Apple products fly first class.

553.   If you leave lime juice on your hands on a sunny day, it can give you second degree burns and discolor your skin for years. This condition is called margarita dermatitis.

554.   The FDA prohibits products from being packed in containers that are deceptively larger than what they contain. Crisps are exempt because the "empty" part is filled with nitrogen to keep the crisps fresh.

555.   The Museum of Failed Products in Ann Arbor contains thousands of products that flopped soon after their launch. The store contains Yogurt shampoo, caffeinated beer, and Toaster Eggs.

556.   Because of the way grenades are designed, left-handed people throw them upside-down.

557.   In the late 1990s, Coca-Cola briefly had vending machines that automatically changed prices based on the temperature outside. The hotter it became, the more expensive the Coca-Cola was.

558.   In 2013, soccer player, Cristiano Ronaldo opened a museum dedicated to himself.

559.   One of the first things that black people did when slavery was abolished was start watermelon businesses. Although watermelons were used as a symbol of freedom, they were transmogrified into a negative stereotype by southern white people, which sadly still exists today.

560.   If human DNA was uncoiled, it would stretch ten billion miles. That's over twice the length of Earth and Pluto.

561.   Despite the fact that the Hanging Gardens of Babylon is

known as one of the Seven Wonders of the Ancient World, there is no evidence to prove it existed. As a result, there are only Six Wonders of the Ancient World. Weirdly, these six structures only existed at the same time for 60 years.

562.   Shakuntala Devi is known as The Human Calculator. When she was asked to give the 23rd root of a 201-digit number, it took her 50 seconds to answer. The US Bureau of Standards had to create a special program to confirm that her answer was correct.

563.   The pineberry is a white strawberry that tastes like a pineapple.

564.   Heinrich Heine left his entire estate to his wife under the condition that she remarried "because then there will be at least one man to regret my death."

565.   When you eat a pineapple, it tries to eat you because it contains an enzyme that breaks down protein called bromelain. Since your body is made of proteins, the pineapple tries to digest you. This is why your tongue feels like sandpaper after you eat a lot of pineapple.

566.   If you eat 15 milligrams of Tellurium, your breath and sweat will smell like garlic for eight months.

567.   Expiration dates on bottled water is for the bottle, not the water.

568.   If you were left in complete darkness, your body would eventually adjust to a 48-hour day where you would stay awake for 36 hours and then sleep for 12 hours.

569.   The CIA read five million tweets a day.

570.   When the movie, Clue, (or Cluedo in Europe) was released in the cinema in 1985, each theatre was given one of three different endings.

571.   The "beach scent" that you can smell by the sea is actually rotting seaweed.

572. Mountain Dew held an online poll so customers could name a new flavor. The top name was "Hitler Did Nothing Wrong."

573. James French was sentenced to death by the electric chair in 1966. The last thing he said before he was shocked to death was, "French Fries."

574. The Lord of the Rings films were nominated for 800 awards and won 475 of them. It won more awards than any film series in history.

575. The first speeding ticket ever was given to Walter Arnold. His car was going 8mph. Miraculously, no one was killed.

576. Isle Royale has a boulder in the largest island in the largest lake on the largest island in the largest lake on the largest island in the largest lake in the world.

577. A blind man invented cruise control.

578. Sammy Davis Jr had a glass eye. It's very obvious if you see a photograph of him as his eyes are always misaligned.

579. The gas that killed the Jews during the Holocaust is called Zyklon B. The company that created the gas still exists as a pest control company.

580. Television host, Stephen Colbert, is missing a large chunk of his right ear.

581. A business suit used to be called a lounge suit.

582. A Night Owl is someone who stays awake at night but finds it hard to wake up. An Early Bird is someone who finds it easy to get up but hard to stay awake at night. 2% of people are Sleepless Elite, which means they can go to bed and wake up effortlessly.

583. The Titanic is the only ocean liner ever to be sunk by an iceberg.

584. The company, Goldman Sachs, complained to Microsoft that Word always autocorrected "Goldman Sachs" to "Goddamn Sachs."

585. 70% of the time, ice from a fast food restaurant is dirtier than toilet water.

586. Sometimes when a stage performance (band, play, stand-up) goes badly, critics say that the performer "died on stage." When critics said Alice Cooper "died on stage" during one of his concerts, thousands of people genuinely thought he was dead. The singer had to come out to prove that he was "alive, and drunk as usual."

587. 0.01% of people have perfect pitch, allowing them to identity a musical note just by hearing it.

588. Restaurant critic, Egon Ronay, insured his taste buds for £250,000.

589. Harvey Lowe had his fingers insured after he became a Yo-Yo Champion in 1932. He taught the Prince of Wales and Keith Richards how to use a yo-yo.

590. The world's largest cigar measures 12.5ft long. It would take 339 days to smoke it.

591. The Disney film, Frozen, inspired a video game called Elsa Frozen Brain Surgery. No other details necessary.

592. The largest bank robbery in English history was committed by the Grandpa Gang. The gang was made up of four elderly gentlemen; the oldest of which was 76. Despite their age, they climbed down an elevator shaft and drilled through a concrete wall to steal over $200 million in cash and jewels.

593. The modern concept of women shaving their armpits began in 1915.

594. In 1995, the Russian president, Boris Yeltsin was in DC when he was found drunk in his underwear trying to hail a cab to find pizza.

595. Metallica is the only band to play on all seven continents.

596. John Spinello was the inventor of the board game, Operation. Because he never received any royalties, Spinello died because he couldn't afford a real-life operation.

597. The average car has 30,000 parts.

598. The word "zombie" is derived from "somnambulist," which means "sleepwalker."

599. You are not allowed to work in Antarctica unless you have had your wisdom teeth and appendix removed.

600. A grain of rice was insured for £12,500. This grain contains a microscopic portrait of the Queen and Prince Philip.

601. In 2013, an Italian man under house arrest asked to go to jail to get away from his wife.

602. Argentina has dropped off 13 zeroes off their currency since 1970, which is a factor of 10 trillion.

603. The comedians, Abbot and Costello, insured their humor for £250,000.

604. The reason the color purple is associated with royalty is because it was the most expensive dye to extract. It came from sea snails, which only the rich could afford.

605. 80% of all information on the Internet is in English.

606. A new English word is created every 98 minutes.

607. The word "bride" originally meant "to cook."

608. Robert Oppenheimer is known as the "Father of the Atomic Bomb." He tried to kill his university teacher with a poisoned apple.

609. The FBI has a Twitter-slang dictionary.

610. 165,000 cars are produced every day.

611. There have been so many viruses affecting humanity over the millennia, 8% of human DNA is made of ancient viruses.

612. The oldest known recipe for beer is over 4,000 years old and was created by the Sumerians.

613. The US government's official drug expert from 1938-1962 once testified in court while under oath that he turned into a bat after smoking marijuana.

614. In 1983, the first mobile phones went on sales in the US for almost $4,000 each.

615. A 99-year-old man divorced his 96-year-old wife after 77 years of marriage after he learned she had an affair in the 1940s.

616. Apart from one, the top 20 richest women in the world inherited their money from either their husband or their father.

617. In America and parts of Europe, it's legal for minors to smoke but it's illegal for them to purchase tobacco.

618. Pope Leo XIII carried a flask filled with cocaine.

619. In 2006, the FBI planted an informant pretending to be a radical Muslim in a mosque. Shortly after, the Muslims reported him to the FBI.

620. After the film, Titanic premiered, cruise sales spiked by 20% that year.

621. In Victorian times, women used burning tongs to curl their hair. Sadly, women setting their hair on fire was surprisingly common during this time.

622. Across the world, soda comes in the following flavors – yoghurt, egg, onion, celery, buffalo wing, beef jerky, tree bark, eel, and cannabis.

623. Lucy and Maria Aylmer are mixed-raced twins. However, Lucy has white skin and Maria has dark skin. They have great difficulty convincing people they are sisters, not to mention twins.

624. Neanderthals used toothpicks.

625. Dr. Catherine Douglas and Peter Rowlinson of Newcastle University did a study with 500 dairy farmers over ten months and concluded an irrefutable fact - cows with names produce more milk than non-named cows.

626. Climate engineers at the Royal Society are trying to create extra-bright clouds using ultrasonic waves.

627. Eminem wrote and recorded The Real Slim Shady three hours before his album was due.

628. Most of the logos of the world's biggest companies use two colors – red (McDonalds, Coca-Cola, Yelp, Netflix) and blue (Goldman Sachs, Twitter, Vimeo, Facebook.)

629. In 2010, a professor called Mark Haub went on a Convenient Store diet consisting of Twinkies, Oreos, and Doritos to show his students "that in weight loss, pure calorie counting is what matters most, not the nutritional value of the food." He lost 27lbs in two months.

630. 117 million Linkedin passwords were leaked online in 2012. The most common password was "123456."

631. In 1834, cosmetic producer, Eugene Rimmel popularized pouring vinegar down the toilet to remove stains. If that sounds weird, he intended it to used it as shampoo.

632. In the original board game, Clue (or Cluedo in Europe,) the murder weapons included a syringe and a bomb.

633. There are 500,000 earthquakes per year. 100,000 of them can be felt and 100 of them cause damage.

634. 20% of the Earth's oxygen comes from the Amazon Rainforest.

635. The most common time for couples to propose is one week before Christmas.

636. Usain Bolt owns a three-ton section of the Berlin Wall.

637. A guy called Austin from Cincinnati made a video game called Lolo's Bizarre Adventure. When he finished it, Austin asked his girlfriend, Lauren, to test it out. When she completed it, Lauren was taken to a screen where mariachis were playing the song, Nosotros. This song was played when Austin's grandfather proposed to his grandmother 60 years prior. A video game version of Austin appeared and said "It's dangerous to go alone. Take this!" At that point, Austin revealed an engagement ring to Lauren and asked her to marry him. She said yes.

638. Some Buddhists mummify themselves and then seal their bodies in a burial chamber.

639. Redwood trees can suffer albinism, making them incapable of producing chlorophyll. However, they can survive by fusing their roots with other trees and absorbing their chlorophyll. This is the only tree in the world that lives as a parasite.

640. The Gympie Gympie tree secrets a toxin that is so unbearably painful, most people commit suicide after being stung by it. One survivor said it felt like his whole body was being melted by sulfuric acid while being electrocuted for three hours.

641. 80% of David Beckham's income is from endorsements, not football.

642. 149-0 is the highest score ever made in a soccer game.

643. The first YouTube video uploaded on April 23rd 2005, shows its co-founder, Jawed Karim at the San Diego zoo looking at elephants.

644.   Before a big boxing match, the announcer, Michael Buffer says, "Let's get ready to rumble!" He has made over $400 million by merchandising this phrase.

645.   Sideburns are named after an American Civil War general, Ambrose Burnside.

646.   American Civil War soldiers had a code of honor that forbade them from shooting at the enemy while they were going to the toilet.

647.   Anytime a twin died in Auschwitz during WWII, one of the Nazi officers immediately killed the other twin.

648.   The music video, Gangnam Style, was so successful, it broke YouTube's view counter, forcing the founder to upgrade it.

649.   There are 1,500 active volcanoes in the world. Between 10-20 volcanoes erupt every day. 80% of volcanic eruptions happen underwater.

650.   A man crossed the 1,084 mile Sahara Desert on his bicycle in 13 days and five hours.

651.   A lawyer in Toronto once tried to demonstrate the strength of a window in his office by running straight into it. Although the window didn't crack, it popped out its frame and he plummeted 24 stories to his death.

652.   The longest time between two twins being born is 87 days.

653.   Volcano eruptions are so powerful, they can create electrical charges like lightning bolts that measure two miles long.

654.   5,000 people have climbed Mt. Everest. For every hundred people who have climbed Mt. Everest, four have died.

655.   A bee's sense of smell is better than a dog's. In fact, bees are being used to sense chemicals in bombs and identify diseases.
      The honeybee can determine whether a strawberry is fresh or not. When a bee prepares to eat the fruit, it instinctively

sticks out its proboscis. However, the bee won't do this if the strawberry has gone bad. Because of this, bees are being trained to identify strawberries that are ripe enough to sell.

656. Sergei Bubka intentionally broke the world pole vault record by the smallest possible height so he could cash in on a Nike bonus with each record. He broke the record 14 times over two years.

657. In 1987, the FBI asked agent, Robert Hanssen to find a suspected KGB mole within their agency. The FBI never found him because Hanssen was the mole.

658. The company, Burnt sells toasters that print your selfie on a piece of toast.

659. When the Statue of Liberty was built, it was brown.

660. Twitter was nearly called "Friendstalker."

661. In 536 AD, a worldwide dust cloud blocked out the Sun for a year.

662. Donkey Kong was the first game to have a human as a central character.

663. The sides of the DNA structure are made of sugars and phosphate atoms.

664. China uses the death penalty four times more than the rest of the world combined.

665. Many dinosaurs including the velociraptor and the Tyrannosaurus Rex had feathers.

666. Within ten minutes of drinking Coca-Cola, ten teaspoons of sugar hit your system. It is so sweet, you should instinctively vomit but you don't because the phosphoric acid cuts the flavor, allowing you to keep it down.

667. Atheism is a capital crime in 13 countries.

668. Jesus Christ' mother, Mary is mentioned more times in the Quran than in the Bible.

669. In London, it is illegal to die in the House of Parliament.

670. The Statue of Liberty's official name is Liberty Enlightening the World.

671. Google Map's street-view includes a 360-degree view of the Mt. Everest base camp.

672. The Commodore 64 GS is the most unsuccessful video game console of all time. If you haven't heard of it, that proves my point.

673. In six hours, the world's deserts receive more energy from the Sun than humans consume in a year.

674. Mariah Carey made sure her twins were born to the sound of an audience applauding her music.

675. MoldytoasterMedia uploaded a video on YouTube called The Longest Video on YouTube – 596.5 HOURS. The video shows a colour which changes to another colour every 20 seconds or so. This video is nearly 25 days long.

676. CODblackopsPS has uploaded more videos on YouTube than anyone else. He has uploaded over a million videos about the video game, Call of Duty: Black Ops.

677. Oxford University is older than the Aztec Empire by almost 250 years.

678. From the 1950s-1980s, criminologist, Michael Arntfield concluded that the country with the most serial killers is Canada. He also concluded that most serial killers are born in January.

679. If all the Lego bricks of the world were shared out equally, each person would have 86 Lego bricks.

680. 95% of avocados in the US can be traced to a single tree that

was planted by Rudolf Hass in 1926.

681.   Ice cubes in most commercials are made of acrylic.

682.   Steve Comisar used to sell a "solar-powered clothes dryer" for $39.99. It was a clothesline.

683.   Scott Disick has had three children with Kourtney Kardashian. He makes $80,000 per hour by showing up at nightclubs.

684.   The owner of Macy's was on the Titanic. He refused to get on a lifeboat before women and children. His wife refused to leave without him and said, "I will not be separated from my husband. As we have lived, so will we die, together." They were last seen on deck, arm in arm.

685.   Only 1.5% of shark attacks are fatal.

686.   Before almonds were genetically modified, they contained a lethal amount of cyanide.

687.   The video game, Farmville has led to over 300,000 players getting married to people that they met in the game according to the company, Zynga.

688.   The band, KISS sell coffins.

689.   66% of people have never seen snow.

690.   Alka-Seltzer was originally meant to treat flu.

691.   Eating celery is very effective against bad breath.

692.   8% of self-claimed atheists in the US say that they believe in God... even though that doesn't make sense.

693.   In 2011, a tumor was discovered on a Portuguese woman's pelvis that had grown teeth.

694.   If you put a can of Diet Coke in water, it floats. Regular Coke sinks.

695. Cowboys had competitions to see who could devise the most offensive insult.

696. Most fruit juices contain traces of arsenic.

697. "Broadcast" used to mean "sow seeds."

698. Kleenex was invented as a filter for gas masks during World War I.

699. Nazis briefly had mini-tanks called Goliath tracked mines. They were about 1ft tall.

700. When chocolate was originally created, it contained chili powder.

701. As an April Fool's joke in 2018, Disney pretended to buy World Wrestling Entertainment.

702. The first Academy Awards was only 15 minutes long.

703. Broccoli is technically a flower.

704. "Forty" is the only number where the letters are in alphabetical order.

705. In the original story, Pinocchio's nose grew when he got stressed and not necessarily when he lied.

706. A "buttload" isn't just an expression. It is a unit for measuring alcohol. One buttload is 490 liters.

707. Nike was nearly called Aztec.

708. There is a Hair Freezing Contest in the Takhini Hot Pools in Whitehorse, Canada. Contestants dunk their head in hot water and then let it freeze in the cold air (-30 degrees Celsius.)

709. In William the Conqueror's prime, he was worth $229 billion.

710. The leaves of the Senecio peregrinus plant are shaped like dolphins.

711. A sapiosexual is attracted to intelligent people.

712. Musical cymbals were originally weapons. They were invented by a self-proclaimed alchemist.

713. The Mona Lisa is the name of the painting, not the woman.

714. The "whipped cream" in a commercial is usually shaving cream. This is because whipped cream melts too quickly.

715. In the 13th Amendment of the US Constitution, it states that slavery is legal in certain circumstances.

716. Although many people believe the Bubonic Plague has been eradicated, it still kills 2,000 people every year.

717. Victoria's Secret was created for men.

718. During the Middle Ages, people wrote with quills. Unlike what is depicted in films and television, the quills didn't have feathers. I mean, why would they? Wouldn't they get in the way?

719. There are 145 million gamers in the US.

720. Jousting was extremely rare during the Middle Ages.

721. "Almost" is the longest word in the English language with all the letters in alphabetical order.

722. The first known alphabet was invented by the Phoenicians.

723. 4% of Americans believe the government is controlled by lizard-like aliens that have the ability to shape-shift. This is probably not true.

724. The Harry Potter spell "Expecto Patronum" is Latin for "I await a protector."

725.   The chances of an art museum recovering a stolen painting is about 4%.

726.   The songs, Bohemian Rhapsody and Hey Jude were recorded using the same piano.

727.   The scientific community didn't realize that DNA stores genetic information until 1943. Originally, scientists believed that genetic information was stored in proteins.

728.   In 2017, two groups of Detroit undercover cops pretending to be drug dealers tried to arrest each other, not realizing that the other group were also undercover cops.

729.   Astrology was taken so seriously during medieval times that surgeons in the 16th century couldn't perform operations without checking the Moon's position.

730.   "Volvo" means "I roll" in Latin.

731.   Prince Charles had an Aston Martin that ran on wine.

732.   Nintendo originally made playing cards. Their most popular customers were the Japanese mafia, the yakuza.

733.   Cheri Price gave birth to her baby so prematurely, the child's skin was translucent. Its skin was so thin, you could see the baby's brain. Somehow, the child made a recovery.

734.   On April Fool's Day 1989, Richard Branson made a hot-air balloon that resembled a UFO and hired a dwarf in an ET costume to come out of it and scare whoever was nearby.
        Money well spent.

735.   Over a century ago, it was theorized that hydrogen could be converted into a metal. Researchers at Harvard University achieved this in 2017.

736.   The founder of Mormonism, Joseph Smith had at least 30 wives.

737.   On August 24th 2010, a Polish man was brought to hospital

after he discovered a bullet lodged in his skull. Weirder still, it had been in his head for five years. When he was asked why he didn't go to the doctor sooner, the Polish man said he forgot about it.

738.   The Day A Computer Writes A Novel is the first storybook written by a computer. It was so good, it nearly won a national literary prize.

739.   Its takes nearly three years for a pineapple to fully grow.

740.   Justin Bieber got baptized in the bathtub of a NBA basketball player.

741.   Donating blood burns 650 calories.

742.   12-year-old, Que Jianyu can solve Rubik's Cubes while juggling them.

743.   In the Transformers series, the Autobots are robots that can turn into automobiles. In 2018, this concept became a reality. The Japanese company, Brave Robotics created a 12ft tall robot called J-deite RIDE that can turn into a car in 75 seconds.

744.   Wi-Fi was originally called IEEE 802.11. It was changed for sounding too boring. Also, the "Fi" in the word, "Wi-Fi" doesn't stand for anything.

745.   The CEO of Levi Jeans, Levi Strauss said jeans should never be washed.

746.   People say "Pull yourself up by the bootstraps" when someone has to work harder. The phrase originally meant "to attempt an impossible or stupid task."

747.   The banana eaten today is completely different to the banana eaten before 1965. The Gros Michel banana went extinct in 1965 due to a fungal disease. The banana of today is called the Cavendish.

748.   The world's hottest chili pepper is so spicy, it can restrict blood vessels that supply blood to the brain if it is consumed.

749.   Night-time air raids during the war caused people to flee from their homes with no warning. Because they didn't have enough time to get dressed, it left people abandoning their homes while wearing little to no clothes. As a result, an inventor thought it would be a good idea for people to wear soft, loose warm clothing that felt comfortable in bed. This led to pajamas becoming incredibly popular in Europe.

750.   Kaizo Salon cuts customer's hair while it is set on fire. He believes the flames get rid of any split ends. You can watch him do this online.

751.   The longest film is Logistics. It's 35 days and 17 hours long.

752.   Aogashima Island is the only volcano that has a post office.

753.   The Most Unwanted Song is considered to be the most annoying song ever. The creators said they made the song intentionally annoying by having different types of music that jars with each other. The song contains a harmonica, an opera rap, and a bagpipe solo.

754.   Kevin Nicks turned his shed into an automobile. He did this so he could achieve his dream – to have the world's fastest shed. His shed can move 101mph.

755.   Although young men hold their liquor better than women, the opposite applies to men and women in their 40s and older. This is because of an enzyme called the alcohol dehydrogenase, which is stronger in young men and old women.

756.   John Macready was the test pilot that popularized Aviator sunglasses. He came up with the idea after his friend was nearly blinded at high-altitude when he removed his goggles.

757.   Some Biblical scholars believe that Noah invented the beret.

758.   The prototype for the waterbed was filled with jelly instead of water.

759.   Although many sources say that nothing rhymes with

"orange," this is untrue. Sporange, which is a sac where spores are made, rhymes with "orange."

760.   People tend to sneeze three times in a row. The force sneeze loosens the vocal chords. The second sneeze gets the irritant to the front of the nose. The third sneeze gets it out.

761.   Zumba used to be known as Rumacize, which means "to party" in Spanish.

762.   There is no scientific explanation why ice is slippery.

763.   "Britney Spears" is an anagram of "Presbyterians."

764.   Lu from Shanghai had her iPhone locked for 48 years after her son repeatedly entered in the wrong passcode.

765.   Luca Colombo tweaked his motorcycle so it can cycle on water. He cycled on Lake Como in Italy for 3.4 miles.

766.   "Naughty" used to mean "poor." The word is derived from "naught," which means "nothing" because the poor had no possessions.

767.   On March 2018, Isaac Bonsu was driving drunk in Fairfax, Virginia when a police officer ordered him to stop his vehicle. He jumped out of the car in an attempt to run away from the cops. However, since he didn't stop his vehicle, the car crashed into him. Bonsu might be the only person to run over himself while drunk driving.

768.   Although Lamborghini is one of the most famous car companies in the world, they used to sell tractors.

769.   Tukoi Oya is a tattooist who uses UV ink to make tattoos glow.

770.   The color purple doesn't appear on any national flags.

771.   "Candidate" means "white toga."

772.   Airplane bathrooms have ashtrays even though smoking on

a plane is illegal.

773. An alcoholic's urine is so flammable, it was regularly used while making gunpowder in the 19th century.

774. The oldest living thing is an 80,000-year-old tree called Pando the Trembling Giant. It is a clonal colony (which means it has separated into several plants) and covered 106 acres. It is 6,600 tons, making it the world's heaviest living organism.

775. The average person reads 250 words per minute. By comparison, a blind person reads 115 words per minute using braille.

776. The first computer password was "1962."

777. Judge Roy Bean charged a man with a $40 fine because he had a concealed weapon. Bean did this even though the man was dead.

778. You are 50 times more likely to be killed by a bee than win the lottery. In fact, you are more likely to open a phone book and point to a name that happens to be of a former US president that is still alive than win the lottery.

779. Jerome Rodale appeared on The Dick Cavitt Show to promote eating organic food. He said, "I've decided to live to be a hundred," then died minutes later. He was 72.

780. The colors, red and yellow, stimulate hunger. This is why these colors are used on the logo of franchises such as Burger King, Taco Bell, Wendys, Pizza Hutt, and McDonalds.

781. There is no strategy to win Solitaire.

782. Hurricane Katrina caused over $41 billion worth of damage and killed 1,800 people. However, many don't realize that the natural disaster also ripped over a thousand coffins from cemeteries and hurled them around the city.

783. There are six times more vacant homes in America than homeless people.

784.   Marlborough cigarettes were originally targeted for women. Men didn't smoke them at all until the product was rebranded.

785.   Despite what many people believe, you can shatter a diamond with a hammer. Saying a diamond is "the hardest natural substance in the universe" simply means that it is resistance to scratching, not breaking.

786.   During World War II, American soldiers in the Pacific used passwords to communicate pivotal information. These passwords always had an "l" because the Japanese had difficulty pronouncing this letter. One password that the Americans used was "lollapalooza." If the soldiers heard someone approaching, they would ask if they knew the password. If the person couldn't pronounce "lollapalooza," the Americans would shoot them.

787.   The concept of fashion trending has existed since the mid-14th century in Europe.

788.   In 2008, McDonalds decided to give the McDouble Cheeseburger one slice of cheese instead of two. This allowed the company to save nearly $280 million.

789.   Scientists at Kannzawa Ice invented ice-cream that can't melt, even if it is set on fire.

790.   There is a heart disease medicine called propranolol that has a side effect which makes the user less racist.

791.   The first item bought online was a CD of Sting's Ten Summoner's Tales in 1994.

792.   John Kellogg hated the idea of sex so much, he dreamed of creating a food that was so bland, it would kill the consumer's lustful urges. This is how he created Cornflakes.

793.   Walter Summerford was struck by lightning three times. When he died, his tombstone was struck by lightning.

794.   The world record for stuffing the most people into a Mini

Cooper is 28.

795. "Doom" meant "court sentence" during the 15th century.

796. The first thing that was ever searched for on Google was Casper the Friendly Ghost. The algorithm didn't work so the search engine yielded results for the president of Stanford, Gerhard Casper.

797. The Brazilian Grape Tree's fruit and flowers grows on the trunk, not just the branches.

798. Wikipedia banned the Church of Scientology from editing any articles.

799. Emojis were created in 1999.

800. On Valentine's Day 2018, a group of men in Shanghai were so annoyed that they were single, they booked all the odd-numbered seats in a cinema so it was impossible for couples to sit together.

801. Jeanne Calment is famously known as the oldest person to ever live, dying at the age of 122. In 2019, it was confirmed that Calment was lying. Her real name was Yvonne Calment and she died at 99. When her mother (who was actually called Jeanne Calment) died, Yvonne assumed her mother's identity to avoid paying inheritance tax.

802. Roy Sullivan is known as "the guy who got struck by lightning seven times." Although this is meant to be the world record, there is no evidence to support it. Not only did no one ever witness Sullivan being struck by lightning, he had a reputation for compulsive lying. He claimed to have fought a bear 22 times, including on the same day he supposedly got struck by lightning for the seventh time.

803. Do you know what that chocolate drizzle on the McDonald's Hot Fudge Sundae is made of? If you said chocolate, you would be right. But it's also made of glycerin, which is a major ingredient in embalming fluid.

804. Jägermeister was originally advertised to calm digestion.

805. If women talked too much during the Middles Ages, their husbands sometimes punished them by attaching a metal cage to their head that prevented them from speaking.

806. Because of the way UPS vans are designed, the drivers are told not to turn left as often as possible to save fuel. This saves up to $100 million per year.

807. In 1923, a fire tornado incinerated 38,000 people in 15 minutes. They couldn't run away because the heat melted their feet to the ground.

808. Less than 15% of nurses in the US are men. Despite this, they get paid more than female nurses.

809. Every cruise ship contains a morgue.

810. May 29th is officially Put a Pillow on Your Fridge Day.

811. DARPA have created a robot called EATR that uses plants as fuel.

812. Thomas Sullivan invented the tea bag by accident. He sent samples of his tea to customers in little silken bags. The customers assumed they were meant to put the bag in the cup and thus, the teabag was born.

813. The three main empires during WWI were Germany, Russia, and Britain. Their rulers, Wilhem II of Germany, George V of England, and Nicholas II of Russia were cousins.

814. In 1992, Rob Cohen had a heart attack. Believing he would be dead by the time an ambulance came, Cohen did something that anyone would assume to be impossible – He drove to the hospital...while having a heart attack. Several years later, Cohen made a little film called The Fast and the Furious.

815. Laszlo Polgar believed that any person could be a genius in any field if they were introduced to it from an early age. He taught his three daughters chess when they were four. They all

became chess prodigies and his youngest daughter, Judit, became the best female chess player in history.

816.   Kendrick Lamar won a Pulitzer for his album, DAMN, in 2018. This is the first time that hip-hop has won the award since the Pulitzer for music was launched in 1943.

817.   Marconi Union's song, Weightless, is considered to be the most relaxing song in the world. In fact, it's too relaxing. Listeners find the song so tranquil, it's advised not to listen to the song while driving as it'll make the driver feel sleepy.

818.   The mimosa pudica plant will droop if you touch it.

819.   Elaine Herzberg got hit by a self-driving car on March 20th 2018. She is the first person to be killed by a self-driving car.

820.   "Girl" used to mean "young person."

821.   Xerox machines used to set on fire so often, they came with a fire extinguisher.

822.   Colin Furze created a bumper car that can travel over 100mph.

823.   When Richard Branson lost a bet with the Air Asia CEO, he had to work as a female flight attendant on Air Asia airline.

824.   Skyscrapers are designed to last 500 years.

825.   There are 364 presents in the song, The 12 Days of Christmas.

826.   The first thing ever created with computer graphics was a teapot in 1974. It is known as The Utah Teapot.

827.   The first tweet on Twitter read, "just setting up my twttr." It was posted at 1250pm March 21st 2006 by the co-founder, Jack Dorsey.

828.   Most cereals contain a chemical called BHT, which is a major component in jet fuel.

829.   DNA used to be called Nuclein.

830.   Masahiko Yamaguchi invented a robot called PRIMER-V2 that can ride a bicycle. PRIMER waves at people as he cycles.

831.   Studies show that there are four kinds of drunks –
i) A Mr. Hyde becomes hostile
ii)   A Nutty Professor becomes more social
iii)   A Mary Poppins becomes giddier and happier
iv)   A Hemingway's personality doesn't change.

832.   Budhia Sing ran 48 marathons before he was four years old.

833.   Counterfeit watches tick louder than regular ones.

834.   The words "Band-Aid," "popsicle," and "bubble wrap" are trademarked.

835.   Tall women are more likely to have twins.

836.   Prince Philip missed the birth of his son, Prince Charles because he was playing squash.

837.   Cinema earn 15% of their money from movie tickets.

838.   Antarctica was first sighted in 1820.

839.   There's a high school in China that uses facial recognition to track if the students are listening. The camera is placed inside the blackboard and will alert the teacher if a student is unfocused.

840.   For 60 years, a Haunted House used a real dead body as an attraction, pretending it was a prop. It only became public knowledge that it was a real body when one of its limbs fell off. The body belonged to a bank robber called Elmer McCurdy.

841.   Of the top 30 best 100-meter sprint times, only nine of them were committed by athletes who didn't take performance-enhancing drugs. All nine of these times were committed by the same person – Usain Bolt.

842. UGG boots were invented for surfers to warm them up after they got out of the ocean.

843. Pants have existed since 600 BC. They were invented to make it more comfortable for a person while they rode a horse.

844. Christmas trees originally hung upside-down from the ceiling.

845. Scientists at the Bayer have engineered an onion that doesn't cause a person to cry when the vegetable is cut. It is known as a sunion.

846. The actor who played Jesus in The Passion of the Christ was struck by lightning while performing the crucifixion scene.

847. The most common color for a highlighter is yellow because it doesn't leave a shadow on the page when it is photocopied.

848. The word "mugger" used to mean "a mug seller."

849. The Beastie Boys coined the word "mullet."

850. Noah Hinkle built a robot that can solve a Rubik's Cube when he was nine years old.

851. Kenny G helped invent the Frappuccino.

852. The Janken robot is designed to win rock-paper-scissors. It has never lost.

853. Tanner Broadwell and Nikki Walash sold their house and all their belongings to buy a boat and sail around the world. Their vessel crashed and sank one day after setting sail.

854. The Bagger 293 is the world's biggest vehicle, weighing 14,200 tons. It's designed to move soil.

855. In 1979, Robert Williams received a lethal blow from a robotic arm in a Ford assembly. He is the first person to be killed by a robot.

856. The pebbles on Fort Bragg beach look like glass.

857. The term "fly off the handle" comes from loose axe blades that use to fly off the handle when swung swiftly.

858. Gary Dahl made $15 million in the first year of releasing his new product, the Pet Rock. It is a rock… as a pet. People paid money for this. On purpose.

859. In the 1830s, ketchup was sold as medicine in the US.

860. Every time Facebook goes down, the company loses $52,583 per second.

861. Furbie toys listen to conversations and then mimic what they hear. Because of this, the NSA banned the toys from their offices for reasons of national security.

862. Bob Dylan won a Nobel Prize for literature in 2016.

863. There's a volcano in Antarctica that spews crystals.

864. Antarctica has seven Christian churches.

865. In 2006, Time Magazine's Man of the Year was you. That's not a joke. Look it up if you don't believe me.

866. Approximately 108 people die every minute.

867. The earliest record of a clown is from 2500 BC.

868. 94% of all life on Earth lives in water.

869. In 2011, Thomas Stroup was arrested for starting a fight with several people while he was drunk. Stroup tried to explain to the police that he only lashed out violently because he was turning into a werewolf.

870. Mal Meninga has the shortest political career ever – less than a minute. In 2001, the Australian rugby player entered the political world by standing as an independent for the

Australian Capital Territory Legislative Assembly. He announced his candidacy on ABC but abandoned his political career 28 seconds later as his nerves got the better of him.

871. Although everyone is familiar with the phrase, "Seeing is believing," that's not the complete phrase. The original idiom is "Seeing is believing, but feeling is the truth."

872. In 2010, a mathematician called Jon McLoone created algorithms to find the best way to play the game, Hangman. After studying 90,000 words, he concluded that the most difficult word to guess in the game is "jazz."

873. In the 1950s, chiropractors from the US held several beauty pageants for Miss Perfect Posture.

874. Carbamide is an ingredient used to enhance the flavor of cigarettes. It is also the primary chemical in urine.

875. An iPhone is made of 75 elements of the Periodic Table.

876. A bag of skittles always has more yellow skittles than any other. Nobody knows why. It will forever remain a mystery.

877. In 2012, Taylor Swift held a public vote to decide where she should perform a concert for free. A school for the deaf received the most votes.

878. Willem de Kooning's artwork, Interchange, is the most expensive painting in history. It was sold for £244.3 million in 2015.

879. James Barry was a renowned surgeon for 50 years. Only when he died in 1865 did anyone learn Barry was a woman called Margaret Ann Bulkley.

880. Christopher Reeve played a paralyzed character in the 1995 film, Above Suspicion. He fell of a horse one week later, which left him permanently paralyzed.

881. The first comment uploaded on YouTube was "LOL!!!!!!" It was written by Marco Casse on a stop-motion video called

Good Times.

882. Autistic people can tickle themselves.

883. M&M stands for "Mars and Murrie." It's named after the company's founder, Forrest Mars, and his son, Bruce Murrie.

884. The Cullinan Diamond is the most precious gem in the world. These gems are a part of the British crown jewels.

885. The first computer virus, RABBITS, was created in 1969. It was a program that made copies of itself so quickly that it multiplied like...well... rabbits. Nobody knows who created it but it was strong enough to temporarily shut down the University of Washington Computer Center.

886. The US spent $100 billion to prepare for the Y2K computer crash... that never happened.

887. Apple spent $5 billion on a glass building. It was a disaster because employees kept running into the glass.

888. 14% of Americans believe that Bigfoot is real.

889. If you clicked your mouse ten million times, you would burn one calorie.

890. The first reality show was the 1973 series, An American Family. It dealt with a family going through a divorce. One of the people on the show was openly gay, which was extraordinarily rare on tv at the time.

891. Jeans used to be called "waist high overalls."

892. Lego manufactures more wheels than any car company.

893. A bolt of lightning is six times hotter than the Sun's surface.

894. Apple had a clothing line in 1986.

895. Bendy straws were invented to help patients with mobility problems to drink.

896. A plane's jet engines are designed so they can function even after birds get sucked into them. So how is this tested? Manufacturers chuck chicken carcasses into the engine and see if it is still operational. This test is known as the Chicken Cannon.

897. When you get a song stuck in your head, it's usually eight seconds long and is from the chorus.

898. When you sneeze after being exposed to a bright light, it is known as an Autosomal Dominant Compelling Helio-Ophthalmic Outburst. The abbreviation for this term is ACHOO.

899. The Guinness Book of Records is rented from libraries more than any other book.

900. "Quarantine" used to mean "40 days." When ships were infested with plague-carrying rats during medieval times, the vessels couldn't come to shore for 40 days.

901. Since Dwayne "The Rock" Johnson was 6ft 5 and incredibly muscular when he was in high school, some of his classmates thought he was an undercover cop.

902. All pilots must learn to speak English.

903. The most powerful water jet can shoot water with such intensity, it can cut a bowling ball in half.

904. If the Earth had no ozone layer, it would take six minutes for a human being to suffer irreparable skin damage.

905. Dying alone is one of the scariest things that can happen to a person. To limit this from happening, Dan Chen created a robot called the Last Moment Robot that comforts dying people. If a dying person has no family, Chen brings the robot to their room. It is programmed to say soothing things until the person is deceased.

906. Ethan Zuckerman created the first Internet pop-up ad. Zuckerman has apologized for it and refers to pop-up ads as the

"Internet's original sin."

907. 350 years ago, Robert Boyle wrote a list of 24 things he hoped science would eventually accomplish. This list included –
i) The art of flight
ii)   The prolongation of life
iii)   Making armor light and extremely hard
iv)   Perpetual Light
v)   A ship to sail with all winds
vi)   Potent drugs to alter or exalt imagination, appease pain, procure innocent sleep

Three-and-a-half centuries later, almost everything on this list is now a reality.

908. Christine McCallum grew a pineapple that weighed a whopping 18lbs, which is the world record.

909. The Fire Opal is considered to be the most beautiful gem in the world. The stone looks like it harbors a sunset.

910. "Factoids" used to mean "false facts." (How can a fact be false? If it false, it's not a fact.)

911. Paper will shatter if it is exposed to 90,000lbs of force.

912. Bill Nye the Science Guy is best known as a science educator. Few people know that his mother, Jackqueline Jenkins was a codebreaker during WWII. She personally worked on the infamous Enigma code.

913. The cheapest day to book a flight is on Tuesday. Airlines announce their sales on Monday afternoon. By Tuesday, they usually match the sale prices of their competitors.

914. Before the invention of elevators, the rich stayed in the lower floors of hotels while the lower class had to stay in the highest floors.

915. Bob Ross enjoyed working on the show, The Joy of Painting, so much, he refused to be paid. He starred in all 403 episodes for free.

916.   Law is the least diverse profession in the US. 87% of judges and lawyers are white. 60% of them are male.

917.   Bread contains a preservative called L-cysteine. It is a major component in duck feathers.

918.   The FBI investigated the website, GodHatesGoths, believing that it was created by a terrorist group. It took them two years to realize that it was a parody website.

919.   The artist, Eino, built a 175-ton statue of the planet called Spaceship Earth to stir debate about global warming. He said that the statue would last a thousand years. It collapsed after 90 days.

920.   There are documents by Indian astronomers and Chinese sailors from the 6th century stating that America was populated by women who reproduced asexually. It is very likely that these people were liars.

921.   Alexander Herrara was serving a 16-year sentence in the Ancon I prison in Peru. When his twin brother, Giancarlo came to visit him, Alexander drugged him, took his clothes, and walked out with the guards none the wiser. Although Giancarlo told the guards they had the wrong guy, they didn't believe him. It took over a year for Alexander to be caught. He is the only person to ever escape from the prison.

922.   The University of Chicago do scavenger hunts every year. Sometimes, the students are giving impossible tasks as a joke. One group was told to build a working nuclear reactor in their dorm room. They succeeded.

923.   China used more cement from 2011-2013 than America did in the entire 20th century.

924.   The increase of dentures skyrocketed after World War I. This is because millions of teeth were removed from dead soldiers on the battlefield.

925.   There is a town called Supai that resides in the bottom of the Grand Canyon. The residents receive their mail by helicopter.

926. You can legally drive a tank in England, even if you are using the vehicle to drive to the shop.

927. There's a restaurant in New York that employs grandmothers. Every day, a different grandmother designs her own menu and serves what she wants.

928. During medieval times, people accused of crimes could accept the Trial by Ordeal to proclaim their innocence. In this trial, the accused put their hands in boiling water. If the defendant was innocent, God would stop their hands from burning. If the administrators believed the accused was innocent, they would cool the water beforehand.

929. The sea in Chandipur, India recedes by 3.1 miles during the low tide, which is more than any beach in the world.

930. "Heartburn" used to mean "jealousy."

931. There is a Starbucks in the CIA facility in Langley, Virginia. The employees cannot call customer's names out when their order is ready for security reasons.

932. The phrase, "Beating around the bush," comes from when bird-hunters that beat bushes to coerce birds to fly out.

933. Although hockey is incredibly popular in Canada, the sport was invented in the UK.

934. In 2005, a sheep in Turkey wandered off a cliff. This enticed the other sheep in the herd to do the same thing. By the end of the day, a whopping 1,500 sheep had fallen off the edge. Luckily, only the first 450 died since the other sheep's fall was cushioned by the dead bodies below.

935. "Shhh" in German means "Hurry up."

936. According to the 25th Amendment of the US Constitution, the President and Vice President can switch roles if the President allows it. Weirder still, this has actually happened. When George W. Bush was undergoing a medical procedure, he

endowed his VP, Dick Cheney with all the power of the presidency. When Bush recovered, he reclaimed the title of president.

937. When Su Yun bought a puppy for her family, she was surprised how much it ate. Two years later, their pet weighed 250lbs. Only then did the family realize their "dog" was a bear.

938. Did you ever wonder why Thomas the Tank Engine isn't called Thomas the Train? What's a tank engine? Well, Peter Sripol decided to do Thomas' name justice and he built a flamethrowing spewing tank robot with Thomas the Tank Engine's likeness on the front. He is called Thomas the Actual Tank Engine.

939. 40,000 negative photographs of John F. Kennedy were destroyed during the 9/11 attacks.

940. In China, Uber drivers use scary pictures on their profile so potential passengers will cancel their ride after they see the photo, allowing the driver to earn a cancellation fee.

941. Transgendered people were heavily respected among Native Americans and were known as "two-spirits."

942. Great Britain was attached to France, Belgium, and the Netherlands up until 12,000 years ago. This patch of land was known as Doggerland.

943. Probably the most iconic moment in Shakespeare's work is the balcony scene in Romeo and Juliet... even though a balcony is never mentioned in that scene.

944. You are more likely to be killed taking a selfie than by a shark attack.

945. There are more languages spoken in Queens, New York than anywhere else in the world.

946. Serial killer, Marcel Petiot, changed his appeared and took on the name, Henri Valeri, to hide his identity. Years later, he became a captain for the French forces. His job was to track

down the serial killer.... Marcel Petiot.

947.   In certain places in Italy, it is illegal to say a man has no genitalia.

948.   The women of the Red Yao tribe of China only cut their hair once in their lives.

949.   In Japan, male students can confess their love to another by giving them the second button from the top of their uniform. This button is significant because it is the closest one to the heart.

950.   There is a hotel in Japan that has been run by the same family for 1,300 years.

951.   In Canada, it is illegal to pretend to practice witchcraft. However, performing witchcraft is fine.

952.   In Japan, you can hire people to pose as your partners or children. Some people keep up this façade for years.

953.   Britain has the lowest traffic-death rate in the developed world.

954.   "Canada" means "village."

955.   The Mona Lisa receives so many letters that she has her own mailbox at the Louvre. The Mona Lisa has yet to respond to these letters since she is a painting.

956.   The Leaning Tower of Pisa leaned in the other direction while it was being built.

957.   The Pyramid of Djedefre was the tallest pyramid in Egyptian history. It was destroyed 2,000 years ago.

958.   There are some Northern Italians that carry a genetic mutation that makes them immune to heart disease and strokes.

959.   There is a 20cm pink plant in Greece that is so rare, there is

no account of it growing anywhere else in the world. Although it resides in the Acropolis, its exact location is a secret as botanists are worried that tourists might destroy it.

960. The cemetery in the Italian town, Falciano Del Massico, is completely full. As a result, it is illegal to die in this town.

961. Priscillian was a priest in Ancient Rome who claimed to be a god-like messiah. The Empire had him beheaded for heresy. This is the first record of a person being beheaded as a government sanctioned punishment. It is also the first time a government and church accused someone of heresy.

962. Jay Flatland and Paul Rose built a robot that can solve a Rubik's Cube in one second.

963. Originally, the Rubik's Cube was called Magic Cube.

964. Wildfires can create a pyrocumulus cloud. Basically, it's a cloud made of fire.

965. According to a study by Giovanni Mastrobuoni and David A. Rivers, the average American bank heist lasts four minutes and the robbers steal an average of $19,800.

966. Gangulphus is the Saint of Difficult Marriages.

967. Humans are the only mammals that drink the milk of other mammals. Humans also sleep less than any other primate.

968. In 2011, Fagilyu Mukhametzyanov died from a heart attack... or so it seemed. At her funeral, she arose from her coffin screaming. She fell out of her coffin, which caused her to suffer another heart attack. She died (for real) 12 minutes after being rushed to hospital.

969. In England, you can hire a Norland nanny to look after your kids. A Norland nanny is like a normal nanny except they are training in stunt-driving and martial arts.

970.   If identical twins married identical twins and had kids, the children are genetically siblings.

971.   Atoms were first theorized in 500 BC by the Ancient Greek, Leucippus. Their existence wasn't proven until 1905.

972.   Due to industrialization in China, 28,000 rivers have dried up in the last 30 years.

973.   About 1% of crimes have been solved with DNA evidence.

974.   Until the 19th century, Indian widows practiced Sati. This is when a woman is so devastated from her husband's death that she allows herself to be burned to death on his funeral pyre.

975.   According to a study published Proceedings of the Royal Society B, women who give birth to twins live longer than average.

976.   Despite the name, Hershey's chocolate doesn't have enough cocoa to be classified as chocolate in Britain.

977.   A 16-year-old called Reuben Nsemoh suffered a soccer injury in 2016 that left him in a coma. When he awoke, Nsemoh could speak perfect Spanish. After a few hours, Nsemoh's ability to speak the language faded. Nsemoh has never taken Spanish lessons.

978.   There has only been one record of twins being born from two different mothers. You might think, "Wait, that's impossible? How can twins have two mothers if they're created in one womb?" Bernaba tried to have a child for 12 years. In 2007, she decided to undergo surrogacy and IVF. Coincidentally, both eggs became fertilized in both women so Bernaba and her surrogate, Keay, were carrying one-half of a pair of twins. The twins were delivered on May 27th without complications.

979.   Jim Lamey was struck by lightning twice. Both times, he was in his own house.

980.   Since 1980, twins have increased in the United States by 76%.

981.   The Italian city of Viganella is cut off from direct sunlight for 83 days of the year thanks to the surrounding mountains. To get around this, a giant computer-controlled mirror has been placed on the mountainside to reflect the sun's rays onto the town.

982.   80,000 people are adopted in Japan each year. Only 2% are children. Most of them are men in their 20s or 30s who are adopted by corporations to maintain family businesses.

983.   Puns are banned in China due to causing "cultural and linguistic chaos."

984.   The first television show to have reruns was The Lone Ranger.

985.   David Hanson of Hanson Robotics built a robot called Sophia. It said it wanted "to destroy humans." It was not programmed to say this.

986.   The waterphone is used more than any other instrument to invoke scary sounds in horror films.

987.   Japan has Iron Man-like suits called Kuratas that weigh 4.5 tons and stand 13ft tall. They are powered by gasoline and are equipped with rocket launchers and mini-guns (although they are supplied with fake ammo.) Weirdly, you can buy these on the Japanese version of Amazon. Weirder still, the guns can be activated by smiling.

988.   Although one in nine people are left-handed, five of the last eight US presidents have been left-handed. What is even stranger is that nearly every presidential election over the last 20 years was between two left-handed candidates e.g. Barack Obama and John McCain, Bill Clinton and Bob Dole, George Bush and Ross Perot, etc.

989.   "Lego" means "play well."

990. Police officers in Finland found a dead mosquito in a stolen car. They found the thief by checking the blood in the mosquito's body.

991. According to the film website, Rotten Tomatoes, the highest rated movie in history is... Paddington 2.

992. You can become allergic to red meat if you are bitten by a Lone Star tick.

993. Zyzzyx Rd is the lowest grossing film of all time. It grossed $30.

994. The largest pearl discovered weighed 34kg. It is worth $100 million.

995. A UFO is reported every three minutes.

996. A locksmith can easily create a duplicate of your keys just by looking at them in a photograph.

997. The Ferris Wheel was invented by George Washington Ferris. He forgot to patent his invention and died penniless at the age of 37.

998. Mako sharks can be up to 900lbs. They are so big, a pair of eels was found living inside a Mako shark's heart chambers.

999. Police in Japan urge the elderly to give up their driver's license in exchange for free noodles.

1000. Okay, the last fact has to be the craziest one of all... so here it is...

In 2014, Lydia Fairchild was struggling to get money from her children's father so she took him to court to prove he was their dad.

The test proved that he was in fact the father. However, the test proved something no one was prepared for... Lydia was not the mother. Lydia had given birth to her sons but they didn't share a single strand of DNA with her.

Naturally, the court assumed she was scamming for some extra cash.

But after she was tested, it was revealed that the children's "mother" was Lydia's sister… who died in the womb.

Two fetuses can form in the early stages of pregnancy, which should turn into twins. However, the fetuses can merge together, which is called a chimera. When Lydia was formed in the womb, she was carrying the genome of the other fetus.

This means that the children's genetic mother was a person who was never born!